P9-BJP-740

Psalms of Praise: Words of Life
From The Songs of Israel

Frances Hogan is a Catholic scripture teacher who is working as a lay missionary in the Church. She has taught Science and Scripture in West Africa and Ireland for nine years. Since 1975 she has worked full-time as a lay missionary, giving scripture courses, retreats, and working in parishes opening up the scriptures to the people.

Frances Hogan has committed her life to making the Word of God known to lay people in the Church in order to deepen their prayer life and commitment to Christ. She has made a series of Scripture Tapes on books of the Bible and on various spiritual themes.

*Available from HarperCollinsReligious
by the same author*

Christian Essentials Series

Called to Holiness
Choose Life!: The Two Ways
Forgiveness: The Glorious Face of God
Suffering: The Unwanted Blessing

Frances Hogan

Psalms of Praise:

Words of Life
From The Songs of Israel

Fount
An Imprint of HarperCollins*Publishers*

First published in Great Britain in 1986 by Fount Paperbacks
Second impression July 1991

Fount Paperbacks is an imprint of
HarperCollinsReligious
Part of HarperCollinsPublishers
77—85 Fulham Palace Road, London W6 8JB

Copyright © 1986 Frances Hogan

The Author asserts the moral right to be identified
as the author of this work

Printed and bound in Great Britain by
HarperCollins Manufacturing, Glasgow

A catalogue record for this book is available
from the British Library

Conditions of Sale
This book is sold subject to the condition
that it shall not, by way of trade or otherwise,
be lent, re-sold, hired out or otherwise circulated
without the publisher's prior consent in any form of
binding or cover other than that in which it is
published and without a similar condition
including this condition being imposed
on the subsequent purchaser

For Delia and Michael Wynn Jones,
In gratitude for their generous love and support over the past few years. "In return, My God will fulfill all your needs, in Christ Jesus, as lavishly as only God can" (Philippians 4:19).

Acknowledgements

The author acknowledges the help of the following authors:

Weiser, A., *The Psalms. A Commentary*. SCM Press, London, 1962

Kidner, D., *Psalms*, Vols 1 and 2. Inter-Varsity Press, London, 1975

Stuhlmueller, C., *Psalms*. Vols 1 and 2. Michael Glazier Inc., U.S.A., 1973

Sabourin, L., *The Psalms: Their Origin and Meaning*. Alba House, New York, 1974

Scroggie, W.G., *Psalms*. F.H. Revell Company, New York, 1973

The biblical quotations are generally taken from *The Psalms: A New Translation* copyright © The Grail (England) 1963, published by William Collins Sons & Co. Ltd, Glasgow, and used by kind permission.

Other translations referred to occasionally are:

J. B.   Jerusalem Bible
N. A. B. New American Bible
N. I. V.   New International Version
R. S. V. Revised Standard Version

Contents

1

Psalm 1:
The Two Ways

Psalm 1 forms the official introduction to the Psalter, the Book of Praises. It lays down one of the fundamental teachings of all Scripture, namely, that God has given us free will and a choice of paths in life. We are completely free to choose one path or the other, but each of us must live out the consequences of our choice. This may not sound very revolutionary, yet the history of mankind has been written in blood as a consequence. Everyone seeks happiness, but many people do not know where it is to be found. Psalm 1 clearly points the way for those who are lost.

> Happy indeed is the man
> who follows not the counsel of the wicked;
> nor lingers in the way of sinners,
> nor sits in the company of scorners
> but whose delight is in the law of the Lord
> and who ponders his law day and night
>
> (vv. 1–2).

The psalm aims at showing us that only God's people who walk in the path of holiness know what true happiness is. The reason why the path of righteousness, or holiness, is offered to us is so that we shall find true happiness. The whole of Scripture testifies to this. Jesus began His redeeming work on earth by describing true happiness in the Sermon on the Mount. "How happy are the poor in spirit; theirs is the kingdom of heaven. Happy the gentle: they shall have the earth for their heritage. Happy those who mourn: they shall be comforted. Happy those who hunger and thirst for what is right: they shall be satisfied. Happy the merciful: they shall have mercy shown them. Happy the pure in heart: they shall see God. Happy the peacemakers: they shall be called sons of God. Happy those who are persecuted in the cause of right: theirs is the kingdom of heaven" (Matthew 5:3–10; J. B.).

St Paul takes up the same theme in Philippians 4:4 when he says: "I want you to be happy, always happy in the Lord. I repeat, what I want is your happiness" (J. B.). The N.A.B. and N.I.V. use the word "rejoice".

Those who choose God's way know true joy in their hearts.

True happiness was experienced by Adam and Eve before the fall. Sorrow, misery and suffering were the consequences of their choice to go their own way, disregarding God's will for them. The authors of Genesis symbolized this choice in the Tree of Life, which represented the good path; and the Tree of the Knowledge of Good and Evil which represented the "wicked" way, or the way of self-will (Genesis 2:17). The Tree of Life was the choice of surrender to God's will in all things, a life of humble obedience to God's superior wisdom. The Tree of the Knowledge of Good and Evil represented moral autonomy on the part of mankind, the choice to decide what was good or evil in independence of God.

The sons of Adam show this choice clearly: Abel chose surrender to God while Cain chose self-will, the result was his killing of his brother when it seemed "good" to him to do so. (This introduces Psalm 3 which tells us that the good suffer at the hands of the wicked.) The rest of the Bible shows us how individuals and nations make this fundamental choice with all its consequences.

Before entering the Promised Land Moses clearly presented the two ways to the Chosen People, so that their choice for or against the way of holiness would be clear. (See Deuteronomy 30:15–20) "See," he said, "I set before you today life and prosperity (The Tree of Life), or death and disaster (The Tree of the Knowledge of Good and Evil). If you obey the Commandments of the Lord . . . you will increase in the land . . . but if your heart strays . . . you will most certainly perish . . . choose life then! Live in the love of God, obeying His will, listening to His voice, and clinging to Him" (Deuteronomy 30:15–20; N.A.B.). Every child of God is called upon at some stage in his life to make this same choice. Jesus put the challenge clearly to us: "Enter by the narrow gate. The gate that leads to damnation is wide, the road is clear, and many choose to travel it. But how narrow is the gate that leads to life, and how rough the road, and how few there are who find it!" (Matthew 7:13–14; N.A.B.).

This first stanza of the psalm tells us where the righteous will never be found, for it is the way of sin, the path of self-destruction. He will not be found following the advice of sinners for he is walking with God, and therefore will follow God's counsel in the Holy Scriptures. Since the holy person hates sin, his aims and purposes in life will be in contrast to those of the evil doer. He will not be found standing or lingering in the way of sinners, for thus he would be led to follow their example, which would destroy his relationship with God. The worst sin for him would be actually to sit in the meetings of scoffers, and participate in their mocking and ridiculing of all that is sacred. Those who mock God and the sacred show that they are separated from Him; their blind arrogance makes them set themselves above religion and even above God Himself. When young people hear adults mock what is sacred it undermines the very foundations of their faith, and removes what would have been their greatest strength in adult life. Mockery is a deadly weapon to use against religion. Only those who are strong in the Lord will be able to hold out against it.

The righteous person finds his happiness through surrender to the will of God as manifested in His Word. He will therefore be a person of prayer, seeking God with all his heart. He will also be a student of Scripture, for thus he will know and understand clearly God's direction for his life. This contrasts with the sinner who rejects God and His Word, and lives in rebellion against Him. The righteous person discovers that real joy and freedom result from an ever deepening surrender to God's will, for we are eventually set free from all fear, all evil and, finally, all self-seeking. This is happiness.

> He is like a tree that is planted
> beside the flowing waters,
> that yields its fruit in due season
> and whose leaves shall never fade;
> and all that he does shall prosper
> (v.3).

The meaning and value of a life of holiness is shown here in the image of the tree growing tall and strong because it is growing beside a constant supply of water, which is a symbol of grace or divine life. It has nothing to fear from the dreadful droughts of summer which would naturally cause it to wither. Its constant supply of water ensures that its leaves never fade. Therefore it produces its fruit at the proper time. Here we see that the righteous person who lives on the abundant food of Holy Scripture and prayer will grow to full stature, and need have no fear of the storms or trials of life; because divine grace is in abundant supply, his house will not fall (see Matthew 7:25).

Like the tree, the righteous person finds the purpose for which he was created, for the true value of the life of holiness is found in God's will, as the law which governs both the inward and outward life. The fruit of this life is recognizable. Matthew 7:16–20 says: "You will be able to tell them by their fruits – a sound tree produces good fruit, but a rotten tree bad fruit. A sound tree cannot bear bad fruit, nor a rotten tree bear good fruit. Any tree that does not produce good fruit is cut down and thrown on the fire—." The good fruit of a life of holiness is as obvious, therefore, as the bad fruit of a life of sin. All that the righteous person does in obedience to God's will will prosper. The good works of a saintly life are good indeed!

> Not so are the wicked, not so!
> For they like winnowed chaff
> shall be driven away by the wind.
> When the wicked are judged they shall not stand,
> nor find room among those who are just;
> for the Lord guards the way of the just
> but the way of the wicked leads to doom
>
> (vv. 4–6).

If the nature and value of the lives of the holy and the wicked can be grasped and understood in their lifetime, how much more easy it is to contrast them as we look to the future and the ultimate fate of both, as we see God sit in judgement and pronounce the verdict. The winnowing of the chaff is frequently used in Scripture to denote God's judgement (see Hosea 13:3, Zephaniah 2:2, Isaiah 29:5, Psalm 35:5, Matthew 3:12). The sheer lack of substance in the life of the wicked, the absence of anything of permanent value, shows that they cannot last. Their lives will fade out, leaving nothing for others to cherish or follow. Ultimately it is only when they stand before God in judgement that the wicked will realize the utter futility of their lives. But it will be too late then. And they must witness God's approval and protection of the righteous ones. If their eyes had been open they would have seen that God's Fatherly hand had guided the righteous all their lives, and not just when judgement came.

The psalm views life purely from God's viewpoint. The unbelieving world would never agree with this assessment. God is present in everything that is done according to His will, and it is He, not man, who gives the quality of

15

permanence and stability to our lives. Anything done apart from God is doomed to perish (see John 15:5 – "Cut off from me you can do nothing"). Psalm 1 is, therefore, a fitting introduction to the Psalter, inviting all of us to a life of faith and obedience to God's will as the things that really matter.

2

Psalm 2:
The Messianic Drama

Psalms 1 and 2 are closely linked as an introduction to the Psalter. Psalm 1 begins and Psalm 2 ends with a "beatitude", while Psalm 2 begins where Psalm 1 ends, with a threat. Psalm 2 also introduces the messianic prophecies which are scattered throughout the Psalter. Jesus Himself guided the early Church to look for the prophetic level of the psalms: ". . . everything written about me in the Law of Moses and the prophets and the Psalms must be fulfilled . . ." (see Luke 24:44; N.A.B.).

Both Jewish and Christian interpreters agree that this psalm is messianic, like Psalm 110 which closely resembles it. Acts 4:25 attributes the authorship to King David, and it seems to have been used for the ceremony of the enthronement of a king.

In the ancient world, when a ruler died it set the surrounding states in commotion, especially if they were vassals of the dead king. These subordinate regions took the opportunity to revolt in an effort to achieve their freedom. Thus the primary role of the new king was to suppress this revolt in order to consolidate his power and establish peace again. This familiar scene forms the background to this dramatic poem. In fact the whole psalm could have been recited by the new king on his coronation day. The king in question would be of the dynasty of David, and therefore of the House of Judah in Jerusalem. The kings of Judah were God's anointed ones, and so God Himself would suppress any revolt against them. The kings of the earth are warned to submit to God.

If this psalm were to be interpreted on one level, referring only to the kings of Judah, then it is a proud arrogant boast; these were merely petty kings compared to the great empires of the day. When the psalm is read on the prophetic level, however, it contains no exaggerations, and the extent of the prophetic vision can be appreciated.

> Why this tumult among nations,
> among peoples this useless murmuring?
> They arise, the kings of the earth,
> princes plot against the Lord and his Anointed.
> "Come, let us break their fetters,
> come, let us cast off their yoke"
>
> (vv. 1–3).

The various renderings of verse 1 speak of a tumultuous gathering of the nations in revolt against God and His Anointed One, the Messiah. The "why" is very important, for the psalmist sees it as futile, ridiculous and impotent. Opposition to God and His Messiah are both very old and continuous. History abounds with references to persecutors and political systems which have tried in vain to eliminate God and His Christ from the earth. In our own day we have, in the West, freedom of worship, yet the pressure of godless solutions to problems and anti-Christian atheistic humanism weighs heavily upon us.

Jesus, the Messiah, experienced the raging of men against God when Herod and the people of Israel combined with Pontius Pilate and the Gentiles to kill Him (Acts 4:25–26). They failed because He triumphed over death. The nations will not succeed against the Church either, for Jesus promised that the gates of Hell would never prevail against it (see Matthew 12:18).

The enemies of God belong to two classes: some, like the kings and governments, know what they are doing. The masses of people, who often follow their leaders blindly in ignorance of the issues at stake, would be shocked to find that they can be in the other class (see Luke 23:24, Acts 3:17, 1 Corinthians 2:8).

Since Jesus and the Father (Yahweh of the Old Testament) are one, then to oppose God and to oppose Christ are the same thing (see John 10:30, 14:9, etc., Matthew 10:40). Those in revolt want "to break their fetters and cast off their yoke". The discipline of the Christian life and its lofty moral standards are seen as intolerable burdens, and they fight for the right to throw them off. The authority of Christ is denied and the authority which He passed on to the Church cast aside as irrelevant, old-fashioned, conservative and constricting, certainly unsuitable for our times! If only we would study history and learn its lessons, we could see that this cry is as old as the first revolt against God.

It is the assertion of Christ and His Church, that He has sovereign rights to rule over us as King, that is rejected (see Matthew 21:37–38). There would be no problem if Christ and His Church merely gave us doctrines to learn and did not demand any moral conduct to accompany them. The gentle yoke that Christ has demanded of us in Matthew 11:28 is the sweet burden of loving the neighbour, explained in John 13:34. Love of God and neighbour are unknown to those in revolt. Hate would be closer to their condition than love. It is the same for us as it was for Israel; Jesus was set before us as "a sign that would be contradicted . . . so that the thoughts of many hearts would be revealed" . . . in every generation (see Luke 2:34–35).

> He who sits in the heavens laughs;
> the Lord is laughing them to scorn.
> Then he will speak in his anger,
> his rage will strike them with terror.
> "It is I who have set up my king
> on Sion, my holy mountain"
>
> (vv. 4–6).

This revolt against God is ridiculous; it is like a fly attacking an elephant, or a person trying to pull the sun out of the

19

heavens. We may shout and scream at the stars, but they continue their course. God is said to laugh at man's impotent rage because it is so futile. The description is that of an oriental king reacting to the news that some servants were challenging the might of his empire. One stroke of his whip or of his pen and the servants would be wiped out.

To say that God laughs is to ascribe a human emotion to Him who is pure spirit. It is merely an attempt to say in human language how futile it is to revolt against the Maker and Ruler of the Universe. If God were to act in judgement on the nations He would strike terror into the hearts of His enemies, and maybe of His friends too! A powerful meteor striking the earth, or a huge volcanic eruption, or the melting of the icebergs, would cost God nothing in terms of power, but what would it cost us in terms of fear?

Like it or not, God has sent us the Messiah in Jesus of Nazareth, and He is already declared both Lord and Christ (see Acts 2:36). His future coming in glory will be a major shock to the nations of the earth, for what God decrees He performs.

> (I will announce the decree of the Lord:)
> The Lord said to me: "You are my Son.
> It is I who have begotten you this day.
> Ask and I shall bequeath you the nations,
> put the ends of the earth in your possession.
> With a rod of iron you will break them,
> shatter them like a potter's jar
>
> (vv. 7–9).

It is this section of the psalm that could not be applied to any earthly ruler, no matter how great. God never said to anyone but His Only Begotten Son, Jesus, those wonderful words: "You are my Son". This was the anointing and consecration of Jesus as King of Kings and Lord of Lords (see Hebrews 1:5–14). Israel, as a nation, was called God's "son" in the Old Testament. This referred to her election and her friendship with God (see Exodus 4:22). David's descendants were to be considered "sons" in a special sense because they were the anointed kings (2 Samuel 7:14). Jesus alone is Son by eternal generation from the Father (see Luke 1:35, Matthew 3:17, Mark 9:7, 2 Peter 1:17). It is to Jesus, therefore, that the nations were given as His heritage. After the Resurrection He commissioned His representatives to go to the ends of the earth to establish the Kingdom of God. He therefore claimed this right to rule the nations. We see this clearly stated in Revelation 2:26: "To the one who wins the victory – I will give authority over the nations – the same authority I received from my Father" (N.A.B.) (see also Revelation 12:5, 19:15–16). Nothing that man can do will hinder the final triumph of the Gospel.

> Now, O Kings, understand,
> take warning, rulers of the earth;
> serve the Lord with awe
> and trembling, pay him your homage
> lest he be angry and you perish;
> for suddenly his anger will blaze.
>
> Blessed are they who put their trust in God
> (vv. 10–12).

The only hope for the nations of the earth lies in submission to God. They are invited to submit now, so that they may know the joy and peace of the Kingdom of God on earth. "Be wise and be warned" is the tone of the message, for there is no refuge for us outside of God's Kingdom. To reject both love and mercy from God exposes us to His role as the just judge of the world, so the nations are warned both as to their danger and their duty. They are asked not to disregard wisdom in their decision making. To serve the Lord with awe and trembling is a recognition of His majesty. This is that reverential fear that is one of the gifts of the Holy Spirit.

21

The final beatitude can be understood only by those who have lived under God's loving care. They are, literally, to be envied if they have discovered the wisdom of a life of total trust in God, for then they know lasting peace, inner strength when times of difficulty come, and they have found the true meaning of life. Their life is one of quiet joy, a joy which is independent of circumstances, and therefore lasting. They are the truly happy.

3

Psalm 3:
The Hour of Suffering

Psalm 3 was written by King David at a traumatic moment in his life. His son Absalom had led a revolt against him, and had succeeded in winning over most of Israel to his side. To prevent Absalom attacking Jerusalem and putting its inhabitants to the sword because of their fidelity to their king, David decided to flee, taking his immediate family with him. He was accompanied by six hundred soldiers who refused to join the revolt. As he approached the Mount of Olives, he was barefooted like a pilgrim, weeping and with his head covered – signs of mourning (see 2 Samuel 15:7–23, 30–37). Never had Jerusalem witnessed such a scene: the sweet singer of Israel and the mighty commander of armies reduced to this pitiful state at the hand of a rebellious son. Of course David could easily have quelled the revolt, but he would not raise his hand against his own son, whom he loved dearly.

That same night the conspirators decided to move against David with twelve thousand men. David's force would be no match for such an army (see 2 Samuel 17:1). Sadly this trial had been prophesied by Nathan, as a punishment from God for David's adultery with Bathsheba and the murder of her husband. "I will bring evil upon you out of your own house. I will take your wives while you live to see it, and give them to your neighbour. He shall lie with your wives in broad daylight. You have done this deed in secret, but I shall bring it about in the presence of all Israel . . ." (2 Samuel 12:11–12). The fulfilment of this prophesy came when Absalom slept with his father's concubines in the sight of everyone! (2 Samuel 17:20–23).

Because David viewed this revolt as something permitted by God he did not fight; instead he turned to God in prayer with humility and confidence, asking God to deliver him in his time of trouble. David thought that if God permitted the trial, then He would see him through it. He only had to seek God's will and obey, and what God wanted to accomplish in himself and anyone else concerned would come about. Reminded of his own sinfulness, he threw himself all the more onto God's mercy. This action on David's part is a great lesson to all of us; so many people use their sinfulness as an excuse to stay away from God, and never know from their own experience how merciful and loving He is. You might say that this is contradicted by the prophesy above, but no. That prophesy merely says – in our modern words – that there are unavoidable consequences to our actions. David's bad behaviour as a father on the earlier occasion would have influenced the behaviour of his son, who would look to his father for an example in life.

> How many are my foes, O Lord!
> How many are rising up against me!
> How many are saying about me:
> "There is no help for him in God."
>
> But you, Lord, are a shield about me,
> my glory, who lift up my head.
> I cry aloud to the Lord.
> He answers from his holy mountain
>   (vv. 1–4).

There are moments in our lives when we feel abandoned, alone, near to despair. Events can overtake us where we find ourselves misunderstood, even rejected, by those we would have turned to for support. It may seem that even those closest to us have become our enemies, in the sense that they are against us. How terribly lonely is the pain if the trouble has come, as it did for David, as a result of our own weaknesses. Yet how often it happens that we are the authors of our own pain! We can work our way into burnout or even breakdown; we can drink ourselves into the gutter, or we can work for the breakdown of our relationships through unforgiveness. Yet none of us want to overhear our friends say that we are beyond help. That we are finished! David heard them say that even God could not help him.

Gradually we learn, in the midst of darkness and distress, to turn to God in real faith and begin to look for His protection (His shield). We learn through the bitter experience of failure genuinely to rely on God for His help, His mercy and His forgiveness. We look to Him for His love, healing and strength. Like our mother Eve, we too "bring forth" only in pain. Oh, how we cry out against having to lean on God! We will lean on anything and anyone but Him. We lean on our own strength until we find this gets us nowhere, then we lean on others and their wisdom. We lean on theories from books, anything, in fact, but the only One who can really set us free. It is often only when the world turns away from our problems that we discover who our real friend is. We turn to prayer, even through tears of despair, and find Him waiting, the One who is our faithful and true friend, often our only friend in time of need. He does not walk away from the sight of our "leprosy", our sinfulness (see Mark 1:41).

I lie down to rest and I sleep.
I wake, for the Lord upholds me.
I will not fear even thousands of people
who are ranged on every side against me.

Arise, Lord; save me, my God,
you who strike all my foes on the mouth,
you who break the teeth of the wicked!
O Lord of salvation, bless your people!
(vv. 5–8).

25

When we turn to God in genuine trust we find that we stop worrying about the problem on hand. Once we fling ourselves into God's arms in utter abandonment, even when the cause of the trouble was our own fault, we can then rest in utter peace and watch God act on our behalf. One of the things that God cannot resist (if I may use human language) is a person coming to Him in utter trust and abandonment. As soon as we give Him freedom to act on our behalf, we see Him become our redeemer. The fact that David slept peacefully, with twelve thousand men looking for his blood, showed that he had truly turned to God and that he had turned to God in truth. It was a saviour David needed, and it was a saviour he got. The Lord always takes care of our real needs when we commit our cause to Him. "Give us this day our daily needs" was a request that Jesus Himself put into the prayer He taught us.

Once God has aroused us to real faith and trust, we call to Him to arise and act on our behalf. How lovely! We think that the idea is ours when all the while His saving grace has been working to bring us to the point where we can pray effectively. The whole testimony of Scripture tells us to call on God as redeemer and saviour and He will deliver us from our "enemies", whatever they are. For most of us the enemy is "within the camp", in the sense that our own faults and sins are our biggest troubles. The Lord will gladly strike down these enemies for us when we ask Him, and He will give us peace. That is why Jesus died for us on Calvary. The God we sinners celebrate on earth is the God of salvation, the One who through love intervened in our history to become incarnate among us in order to deliver us from the power of our enemies. Deliverance can come from God alone.

When David prayed for the downfall of his enemies he was praying against those who had revolted against him. Yet he gave clear instructions to his soldiers to spare Absalom, his son. When the news of victory came to David, after his men had successfully engaged those in revolt, the only question he asked was about the welfare of his son. When he learned that his son was dead he went into mourning (see 2 Samuel 18:5, 29, 19:1–8). Not only that, but we find him forgiving his enemies, and even placing the leader of the revolt at the head of his army (see 2 Samuel 19:12–24). It is important to understand this. In his prayer, David is praying for the justice of God's kingdom to be brought about, regardless of his own worthiness. As God's anointed king and representative, he is responsible for the Chosen People. Thus he is a type or symbol of the Messiah, who is head of the Kingdom of God. He taught us in His special prayer to say to God our Father: "Thy Kingdom come on earth as it is in heaven – and deliver us from the evil one." The salvation of God's people is one side of the coin that has the punishment of the wicked as the other. If God's Kingdom is to be established among us, then the kingdom of darkness and wickedness must be defeated.

For us as Christians, the enemies that we pray against are not human beings. We do not pray for the downfall of anyone. Our enemies are not flesh and blood, but the powers of darkness at war with the Kingdom of God. To pray for the coming of God's Kingdom is to pray for the downfall of evil. Whichever way it is expressed, the request is the same (see Ephesians 6:10–20). The war against sin is waged first in our own lives, so that the Kingdom of God will be firmly established there, then we join forces with all other disciples of Jesus, to fight evil in the world, and so become God's agents in establishing His Kingdom on earth. In this way the God of Salvation can bless His people with peace.

4

Psalm 4:
True Peace of Soul

This lovely psalm belongs to the Davidic collection of the Psalter. In it he speaks to friends and neighbours who are disheartened and discontented because of difficult times both socially and nationally. No indication is given as to the actual circumstances which provoked David to pen this beautiful prayer, in which we see him achieve true peace of soul and tranquillity because of his unshakeable trust in God.

When I call, answer me, O God of justice;
from anguish you released me, have mercy and hear me!

O men, how long will your hearts be closed,
will you love what is futile and seek what is false?

It is the Lord who grants favours to those whom he loves;
the Lord hears me whenever I call him.

Fear him; do not sin: ponder on your bed and be still.
Make justice your sacrifice and trust in the Lord.

"What can bring us happiness?" many say.
Lift up the light of your face on us, O Lord.

You have put into my heart a greater joy
than they have from abundance of corn and new wine.

I will lie down in peace and sleep comes at once
for you alone, Lord, make me dwell in safety

(vv. 1–8).

The psalm begins with a ringing call to God as the redeemer, the One who manifested His true righteousness through His plan of redemption. From the time of the Exodus the people had learned to cry out to God to save them. Their first prayer was for deliverance from Egypt, but as they began to understand the significance of God's intervention there, they realized that the Exodus was a model for any deliverance from any enemy, spiritual or temporal. They had been released from anguish and dangers before; they could throw themselves on God's mercy in the present situation, and find Him as loving as ever. This action of theirs strengthens our faith and enables us peacefully to trust God in the present crisis.

David now addresses the leaders of society in particular: "You men of rank" (N.A.B.). He is amazed at their lack of wisdom and perception. If they allow themselves to be embroiled in political intrigues, and in the web of deception and corruption which is so easy for those in power, with public money at their disposal, then they show the world how foolish and empty they really are. We have abundant evidence in our own day of political "heads rolling" after a bout of vanity and deceit that they hoped would bring them profit. The greater the conniving the greater the fall afterwards.

Those who are wicked and devious know nothing of the wonders that God works for His friends, especially those who are faithful to Him. They know nothing of the joy and peace in the heart, nor of the abundant fruitfulness of the life. They are unaware of deep communion with God or the joy of answered prayer. This is the way that the friends of God can show to the men of the world. If these men of the world do not turn to God to be clothed with heavenly wisdom, then they are greatly disadvantaged, for the least of God's servants is more wise and prudent than they are. The Lord works wonders of grace in all those who come to Him with openness of heart, those ready to learn and to grow; He grants many favours to His faithful friends.

Unfortunately the majority of people are unaware that God wants this intimacy with them.

The first stage of growth is to tremble and sin not. The words of this translation "fear him" are given in most translations as "be angry and sin not", or "tremble (with fear or anger) but sin not". It is all right to feel angry and upset about something, but we must not use that feeling as an excuse to hurt another person physically or verbally. Verbal abuse can be as damaging as physical abuse. This is, therefore, a serious call to think well before acting. If we are to come to know God deeply, we must go to war with sin, and with the self-seeking that underlies all sin. The reason for this is that sin destroys the relationship with God, isolates us from our neighbour and cuts us off from that wisdom which would make us great leaders in society (see Ephesians 4:26–27).

The next stage is to do some quiet reflective thinking and praying, in solitude or apart from others. Combine this with the reflective reading of Scripture, and God will show you a whole new perspective on life. You will quickly see how vain and futile are the things that keep worldly people away from God, and indeed, how petty are the things that keep God's servants back from true greatness. But this is not enough. It must be combined with the offering of true sacrifice to God in our daily lives. The people of Israel offered material sacrifices to God; they thought that nothing unworthy of Him, nothing maimed or blemished, should be offered.

We Christians have the awesome privilege of offering Jesus, the perfect Lamb, to God in the holy sacrifice of the Eucharist each day. Nothing can be greater or more powerful than this. Yet it does not take away our obligation to offer our lives as spiritual sacrifices to God. We, too, must become little "eucharists", and our lives express our thanksgiving to God in the myriad ways of self-sacrifice and self-denial (see Malachi 1:13–14, Hosea 6:6, Hebrews 13:15–16, Psalm 141:2).

Worldly people spend themselves in an endless pursuit of happiness which forever eludes them, for they refuse to seek it in the only way it can be found. "Our hearts are restless until they rest in Thee", is the famous declaration of Augustine, the converted sinner. He had learned, with all the saints, to lift up his eyes to the Lord in prayer, and let the radiant light of God's glory shine upon his life, releasing him from darkness and sin. No one can describe for others what the radiance of the Lord is like: all he can do is testify that it is the place of unutterable peace and joy. Not all the combined pleasures of the world could equal the sense of fulfilment and peace that it gives. The world's pleasures do not give joy or peace; they leave you unsatisfied, restless, craving for more. "But whosoever drinks the water that I give him will never be thirsty; no, the water that I give shall become a fountain within him, leaping up to provide eternal life" (see John 4:14, N.A.B.; also Isaiah 55:1–3).

Because of our deep trust in God we sleep peacefully, utterly serene in the knowledge of His love and divine protection. Not because we are good, but because He is so good to those who seek Him. As we grow closer to the Lord in our personal relationship, we find the words of this psalm take on a deeper meaning; we begin to cry out for deliverance from the greatest enemy of all, the self, which hides in our own hearts. To co-operate with God in the deliverance from self involves deep and radical self-denial in our daily life, but the result is worth all the sacrifice, for it is a permanent peace and joy, regardless of external circumstances, a joy no one can take from us. This leads us, eventually, to lie down in the sleep of death, utterly secure in God's love, and expecting to awake to eternal bliss.

5

Psalm 8:
Man, the Crown of Creation

This psalm of David is everything a hymn should be. It celebrates the glory and grace of God, declares His wonderful works, and relates us and our world to Him, all in a spirit of mingled joy and awe. With great economy of words David contrasts the paradox of God's ways in His unexpected use of the weak and the strong (v. 2), the spectacular and the obscure (vv. 3–5), the many and the few (vv. 6–8); everything begins and ends with God Himself, the One who is over all, above all and within all. The overriding theme of the whole psalm is the greatness of God the Creator.

How great is your name, O Lord our God,
through all the earth!

Your majesty is praised above the heavens;
on the lips of children and of babes
you have found praise to foil your enemy,
to silence the foe and the rebel.

When I see the heavens, the work of your hands,
the moon and the stars which you arranged,
what is man that you should keep him in mind,
mortal man that you care for him?

Yet you have made him little less than a god;
with glory and honour you crowned him,
gave him power over the works of your hand,
put all things under his feet.

All of them, sheep and cattle,
yes, even the savage beasts,
birds of the air, and fish
that make their way through the waters.

How great is your name, O Lord our God,
through all the earth!

(vv. 1–9).

David, so full of reverential awe at the glory of God,
rejoices in His splendour and majesty with words that are
both ardent and intimate. The dynamic power of his words
flows from the blending of these two opposite religious
attitudes. The glory of God, which fills the whole earth, is
sung by His creatures from the cradle to the grave, and
beyond this is taken up by the heavens themselves, so that
all creation rings with the praise of God. The wonder of it
all is that this great God of glory and majesty is OUR
LORD, the One who relates to us in covenant love.

Contemplating the starry sky, David sees the display of
God's handiwork, and acknowledges its beauty and glory,
giving thanks to its Maker. He presents the sceptics and
atheists with the spontaneous praise of children celebrating
the wonders of Creation, and their childlike joy and songs
of praise to their Maker. These pure first stirrings of real
piety must not be disregarded although they lack reflection, for they are a genuine response to the mystery of
the world around, and can awaken the adult to new faith
when he has become bogged down with his own weighty
thinking and reasoning. There is no argument against the
spontaneous response of God's creatures to His presence.
David hears the voice of God in these little children, whose
intuition surpassed the cognition of adults. Here we are
shown that in the little things God is greatest: *in minimis
deus maximus*. In the response of little ones God has raised
up a bulwark against all the rationalist unbelief of adults. In
Matthew 11:25 Jesus gave thanks to His Father for re-

33

vealing the mysteries of the Kingdom of heaven to mere children and for hiding them from the learned and the clever! In His triumphal entry into Jerusalem, when He clearly revealed Himself Messiah to anyone whose eyes of faith were open, the children were the ones who took up the chant which revealed that they recognized Him as Messiah. When the Pharisees demanded that Jesus silence them, He quoted this verse to show that the children had more spiritual insight than they (see Matthew 21:16, Wisdom 10:20–21) (vv. 1–2).

Engulfed by the vast illimitable expanse of the heavens, with its sparkling splendour, David is overwhelmed by the immense greatness of God, Who made all this with "His fingers". How great must God's mind be that could establish the moon and the stars in their places, with laws that governed their whole existence. If David had our knowledge of the number of galaxies, let alone stars, it would be wonderful to hear his comment! As it was, he was confined to what could be seen with the naked eye; yet even that could produce this wonder and praise from him (v. 3).

It is the revelation of God that enables man to get a right understanding of himself. In the Bible this self-revelation of God and man's understanding of himself are intimately connected (see Isaiah 6:1–13). Man only truly understands himself in relation to God. By comparison with God man can see his own nothingness and insignificance, and truly wonder how so great a being could want anything to do with him. This understanding comes only when the finite is confronted with the infinite, the temporal with the eternal, the ephemeral with the everlasting God.

Now we can ask "What is man?" and realize that we are speaking about an earth-bound, weak, mortal creature, set in the vastness of a universe he will never fully understand. But he does not stop there, for this thought could produce paralysing fear. Instead, using that sense of awe and wonder as the starting point of his thoughts, he tries to grasp the miracle of grace involved in his relationship with this great God, who does not think it beneath Him to take care of his needs. The sheer grace of it all can now sink into his consciousness, and we can appreciate the combination of awe and love that permeate this lovely poem, when we see that this same God, before whom man pales into insignificance, is the same from whom we accept the gift, not only of life, but of love, forgiveness and peace (v. 4).

Now that man's position of nothingness before God has been established, we can contemplate the honour and dignity conferred on him by God Himself in the creation, for it was God who constituted man lord of His creation, with power to rule the earth, and have dominion over other creatures (see Genesis 1:28–30). In this sense man shares in God's reign over the earth, and is made in His likeness, insofar as he is allowed to be crowned with glory and honour, albeit subject to God. The dignity conferred on man by God here is very great, for man is allowed to resemble God in a small way (vv. 5–6).

This passage reaches its full glory in its fulfilment by the Son of Man in the New Testament. The Letter to the Hebrews says that it refers to Jesus in His incarnation, where, for a short time, He was made lower than the angels, but now, in His resurrection, is crowned with glory and splendour because He triumphed over death (Hebrews 2:6–9). In 1 Corinthians 15:27 St Paul claims that this shows that all things will eventually be subjected to Jesus' kingly rule, when all His foes will have been overcome. Thus we can join creation and redemption together, with Jesus as the bridge, the One who is the head of creation, and the first-born from the dead, the greatest among men, and yet God made manifest in the incarnation.

David now depicts in attractive detail the extent of man's dominion over the animal kingdom. Man, himself a frail creature, but made in the image and likeness of God, is able to share both in the spiritual and material worlds, and to rule over natural creation. But he does not end there in the contemplation of man's greatness. He goes back to his starting point, to exult in the great glory of God, which keeps man in balance with regard to himself, lest he stray into the murky area of self-glorification which spoils the image of God in him. In his lordship over the earth man best portrays the image of God when he gives humble service, in love, to those in need. In this he shows the face of God to the world; when he glorifies himself he defaces the image of God in himself, and destroys the world also by his sin.

6

Psalm 19:
The Two Books

Some scholars claim that Psalm 19 is a composite of two separate psalms which differ from each other so much in metre, subject matter, mood and language that they could not be composed by the same author. Verses 1–6 present a nature song similar to Psalm 8, while verses 7–11 extol the Law. The Bible attributes the whole work to David. We shall consider it according to its subject matter, as a psalm with two distinct movements. The first is concerned with the broad sweep of God's revelation of Himself in the universe, the Book of Nature; and the second with the clarity of God's self-revelation in Scripture, the Book of the Law, or the Word. The psalm ends with the heart-searching of verses 11–14, as the worshippers respond to both.

The heavens proclaim the glory of God
and the firmament shows forth the work of his hands.
Day unto day takes up the story
and night unto night makes known the message.

No speech, no word, no voice is heard
yet their span goes forth through all the earth,
their words to the utmost bounds of the world.

There he has placed a tent for the sun;
it comes forth like a bridegroom coming from his tent,
rejoices like a champion to run its course.

At the end of the sky is the rising of the sun;
to the furthest end of the sky is its course.
There is nothing concealed from its burning heat

(vv. 1–6).

Believer and unbeliever alike are invited to observe that the starry sky is an eloquent, if silent, testimony to the glory of God. No matter how educated or uneducated we are, the Book of the Firmament is forever open to the one who cares to examine it. It silently declares the presence, the power, the wisdom and the goodness of the supreme being who is its designer and controller. By day we have one version of the story, but we would be ignorant of its mysteries were it not for the revelation of its myriad galaxies at night, when it can be examined even more closely, and delivers up to us some of its secrets.

Anyone examining the heavens must extol the majesty of the creator unless completely blind; we learn about the worker from his "handiwork". This testimony is seen in every part of the earth, so that we are without excuse if we say there is no God. St Paul said that the pagans of his day were without excuse for their atheism and depravity because what can be known about God is "perfectly plain to them since God Himself has made it plain. Ever since God created the world his everlasting power and deity – however invisible – have been there for the mind to see in the things that he has made" (see Romans 1:18–21; J.B.). In Romans 10:18 Paul goes on to re-interpret this verse, saying that God's messengers, namely the Christian missionaries, have gone through all the earth proclaiming the message. These two witnesses leave us with no excuse for failing to acknowledge God. St Matthew declares that the Magi sought and found the Lord by following God's guidance in the heavens, at a time when no other help was available (see Matthew 2:1–12) (vv. 1–4).

David now launches into a hymn in praise of the sun, which dominates the heavens by day and rests at night, according to the scientific understanding of his time. Remembering that the sun was worshipped by millions of people, the psalmist corrects this erroneous notion by declaring that God the Creator assigned the sun its place in the heavens, where it must run its appointed course in obedience to its maker. Thus he demonstrates that the worship of the sun-god is nonsense, while admiring the sun's great power to light up the world and provide heat for all living creatures. The magnificence of the sun is compared to that of a young bridegroom decked out for his wedding, and its power compared to that of the champion runners of the day – this because the glory of the sun is experienced in every part of the earth simultaneously.

To sum up the testimony of this first part of the psalm, we can say that the witness of the heavens is specific, revealing God's wisdom, power and glory. It is also incessant. The firmament which is the residence of the numberless galaxies, shows forth the divine glory by the number, the variety, the brightness and the beauty of its hosts. The days add to this with their warmth and life-giving light and heat, while the nights complete the message with their stillness, solemnity and starry splendour. These inaudible witnesses are universal and are read in the languages of every people on earth. They are God's travelling preachers who show up the nonsense of idol worship. Finally they are glorious witnesses, full of mystery, strength and power, not at all under the control of man. They run their course independently of man, in obedience to their glorious maker. Thus we see that the heavens do indeed declare the glory of God.

The New Testament applies this hymn to Jesus, the sun of justice, the true bridegroom of the Church, the one who enlightens all men who come into this world; the one through whom the full radiant glory of God was made manifest, and through whom the fullness of God's message to the earth was revealed. It is His missionaries who continue to carry this glorious message of light and life to the ends of the earth, so that all peoples will be saved and come to the knowledge of the truth (see John 1:9, Mark 2:19, Hebrews 1:3, etc).

> The law of the Lord is perfect,
> it revives the soul.
> The rule of the Lord is to be trusted,
> it gives wisdom to the simple.
>
> The precepts of the Lord are right,
> they gladden the heart.
> The command of the Lord is clear,
> it gives light to the eyes.
>
> The fear of the Lord is holy,
> abiding for ever.
> The decrees of the Lord are truth
> and all of them just.
>
> They are more to be desired than gold,
> than the purest of gold
> and sweeter are they than honey,
> than honey from the comb
>
> (vv. 7–10).

Verses 7–10 are very close in teaching, even in wording, to the longest psalm in the Psalter, Psalm 119, which is dedicated to the same theme, namely, the power and value of the Word of God revealed in the Law, or the Scriptures. God's law evokes not only admiration and awe, but also a personal response to its lofty moral standards which brings the obedient to true holiness (vv. 11–14).

The Word of God (I am using "Word" instead of "Law" because the Law came to be the written Word, for both Old and New Testament believers), is here described in six different statements – the law, the rule, the precepts, the command, the fear of the Lord, and His decrees. These present different shades of meaning to explain the value of the Word of God to us. The law refers to the comprehensive revelation of God's will to man. The rule (given as "Testimony" in R.S.V. "statutes" in N.I.V., "decree" in N.A.B. and J.B.) is the witness which God bears to Himself, and to what we should be also. Precepts and commandments indicate the precision and authority with which God deals with us, while reverential fear is the human response fostered by the Word. The last name, given in our translation as decrees, is rendered "judgements" in J.B., and "ordinances" in R.S.V., N.A.B., and N.I.V., and refers to God's judicial decisions on man's behaviour and human situations.

No matter what aspect of the Word we consider under the above titles, we are now told that the Law of God is *perfect*; it is without flaws or defects (v. 7); it is *trustworthy*, sure, reliable, so that we can receive guidance for our lives from it (v. 8). It is *upright*, or morally correct, presenting the right path for man to follow (v. 9), it is *pure* and clean, proclaiming *truth* without shadow of error (v. 10). These characteristics of the Scriptures lead us to a deeper appreciation of their worth.

The Word of God is now shown to have six effects upon us. Firstly, it restores the soul, renewing its spiritual life in the same way as food renews the body. It gives wisdom to those who err. It rejoices the heart, while enlightening the inner eye, and offers sure guidance for the duration of life. Lastly, it contains the most precious good known to the psalmist – righteousness. One who lives out the precepts of God, as outlined in Scripture, will reach the goal of life in real holiness and intimacy with God.

> So in them your servant finds instruction;
> great reward is in their keeping.
> But who can detect all his errors?
> From hidden faults acquit me.

From presumption restrain your servant
and let it not rule me.
Then shall I be blameless,
clean from grave sin.

May the spoken words of my mouth,
the thoughts of my heart,
win favour in your sight, O Lord,
my rescuer, my rock!

(vv. 11–14).

The second book which God provides is that of the law or the Scriptures, and is available to anyone who wishes to know God's will in detail. Its value is above the purest gold, and the satisfaction to the soul greater than that which the sweetest honey can give to the body. In these simple images we hear what a marvellous possession the Word of God is, and how privileged we are to have it. The keeping of it brings great reward, for it forms the character according to the mind of God. This produces great inner freedom, and enduring happiness, stemming from the enlarged vision, the sense of destiny, and the clear guidance as to how to reach it.

As God is more interested in our character than our comfort, the Word also warns us not to be seduced by sin, or lured into wrong ways by evil-doers. The Word also produces an enlivened or quickened conscience, for only God can reveal the hidden sinfulness of the human heart. An increased sense of sin goes hand in hand with increased knowledge of God, just as ignorance of sin reveals ignorance of God. The Word is the bridge which brings enlightenment, and since it is available to all, God must hold us responsible for our so-called ignorance of His will, which the Scriptures so clearly reveal.

Lastly, the Word of God produces not only a more sensitive and enlightened conscience, but also a more confident heart. When one comes to know God better, one grows in confidence of His boundless mercy and love, also of His eternal faithfulness to His Word regardless of our sinfulness, and so we pray to Him with ever greater confidence and love. We turn for refuge and help to the only One who could rightly condemn us for our sins, and in utter joy proclaim Him as our everlasting rock of defence.

Taking the psalm as a whole we find a three-fold testimony to the greatness of God. The heavens bear their silent witness, the Word of God gives the written witness, while man himself is the personal witness. It was for his sake that the other witnesses were given, and to him that God revealed Himself personally. Science and revelation, then, bear united witness to God, and they both prepared for the greatest revelation of God in the incarnate Word, Jesus the Messiah. He is God's eternal Word, hidden in the bosom of the Father from all eternity, and made manifest when the Word became flesh in the womb of Mary of Nazareth, yet He it was whose Word brought all things into being at the dawn of creation. The heavens are the works of His hands, and the Scriptures were given to prepare the stunned world for this greatest good news, that the Word would dwell among us and reveal Himself in all His glory. Jesus *is* the presence of God among us, the Word made flesh, to whom both heaven and earth bear witness (see John 1:1–5, 9–18).

7

Psalm 20:
Before the Battle

Psalms 20 and 21 form a pair. Both were composed by King David, Psalm 20 so that his people could intercede for him before his campaigns, and Psalm 21 so that they could give thanks for his successes. The first one is a prayer of intercession, and the second is praise for answered prayer. Both of them have two parts, and together form a complete whole. In the first part of Psalm 20 the people speak first (vv. 1–5), then the king (vv. 6–8), while in Psalm 21 the king speaks first (vv. 1–7), then the people (vv. 8–12). As you read the two psalms, remember that a battle has taken place between the writing of them.

Both of these psalms are prophetic, and both in their deepest sense are messianic, since they point to Him who is the true king and complete victor over all His enemies. As God's anointed, King David was a symbol pointing to the Messiah.

May the Lord answer in time of trial;
may the name of Jacob's God protect you.

May he send you help from his shrine
and give you support from Sion.
May he remember all your offerings
and receive your sacrifice with favour.

May he give you your heart's desire
and fulfil every one of your plans.
May we ring out our joy at your victory
and rejoice in the name of our God.
May the Lord grant all your prayers.

I am sure now that the Lord
will give victory to his anointed,
will reply from his holy heaven
with the mighty victory of his hand.

Some trust in chariots or horses,
but we in the name of the Lord.
They will collapse and fall,
but we shall hold and stand firm.

Give victory to the king, O Lord,
give answer on the day we call
(vv. 1–9).

Taking this psalm on the historical level first, we find the people of God in the sanctuary, which was at this stage situated in Jerusalem. They are present with their king to offer sacrifice to God and to intercede for the king's safety and victory in the forthcoming battle. As the holocaust is offered by the priest, the people pray that God will hear the king's prayer, and protect him with His own person. This is the meaning of the phrase "the name of . . .". As God's presence resided over the Ark of the Covenant in the sanctuary, the people requested that God would give David his heart's desire and accept all his offerings. David's prayer was that he would conquer all his enemies, and make his kingdom secure. The people can now look forward to marching out to victory, planting the banners of both God and king everywhere. They finish their prayer with a resounding "God save the King!", which has been taken up by generations of monarchies ever since as their prayer and expression of loyalty to a reigning king or queen.

At this point a single voice speaks out, most likely that of the king himself. He declares the firm belief of the people that God would indeed save His anointed one, hear his prayer and give him victory from heaven. All the Davidic

kings considered themselves divinely appointed rulers, therefore, worthy of divine protection in a special way. They saw
themselves in a different class to the other kings.
Nevertheless, they found themselves no match for the enemy
who came in great force against them. Their only hope for
victory lay in God's presence among them as their saviour,
and as the lord of battles. If God was on their side they had
nothing to fear, but certain ruin awaited them if they dared go
alone into battle. Their own history illustrated this often
enough (see 2 Chronicles 14:10, Proverbs 21:31). These
verses also remind us of David's encounter with the giant
Goliath (see 1 Samuel 17:45). He was only a boy then, yet he
fearlessly took on the fierce soldier with only the weapons of
faith and trust in God. The psalm ends with the soldiers
marching out to war shouting "God save the King!"

On the prophetic level this psalm deals wonderfully with
God's true Anointed One, the Messiah. From this
perspective the psalm becomes the prayer of God's people
under the old covenant interceding for the victory of Messiah
"in His time of trouble". Jesus spoke of His time of trouble as
His "Hour", the time of His Passion and Resurrection (see
John 2:5, 7:6, 30, etc). Without realizing it, the people pray
that God the Father will protect Jesus in that dreadful hour of
conflict, which He had to face alone. From His sanctuary in
heaven God will accept the holocaust of His life for us, given
out of perfect love. The psalm renders the sacrifice or
holocaust in the singular, thus allowing for its perfect
fulfilment on Calvary. Surely now God will grant Jesus His
heart's desire, which, unlike David, did not concern Himself
or His own prestige. Jesus wanted all men and all nations to
be saved and to come to the knowledge of the truth. He
revealed His heart to us in His priestly prayer in John 17:
"Father . . . . that he may bestow eternal life on those you
gave him . . . that all may be one as you, Father, are in me,
and I in you; I pray they may be one in us, that the world may
believe that you sent me" (John 17–3; N.A.B.).

The request that follows is now very significant: "May God

grant all your prayers! Unknowingly the people co-operate with Messiah in His prayer for their redemption, which, if they but understood it, would be their own heart's desire too. Now as one voice the people of God assert their belief that God would indeed save Messiah in His time of need. The prayer is not to save Him *from* death, but to save Him *through* death, so that His passover would be, for Him first, and for all of us later, a real passing over from death to eternal life, happiness and peace. This is the ultimate victory. The psalm ends with the people asserting the kingship of Messiah and praying for His glorious reign.

Looked at from this angle the psalm leads us to contemplate Jesus in His passion and to see His glorious hour on Calvary as the centre of all time, with the Old Testament praying for Messiah as He goes towards His hour, and the people of the New Testament giving glory to God for His victory in Psalm 21.

On the subject of prayer itself, this psalm teaches us the importance of praying for each other. We have a duty to pray for those in government over us, so that God will give them the wisdom they need to rule the nation for the common good, and more importantly that the will of God for that people be carried out. The greater the responsibility, the greater the need for support in prayer (see 1 Timothy 2:1–3).

Furthermore, the intercession shown in this psalm is not that of an individual, no matter how holy. It is the whole company of God's people gathered in prayer as one body, with their rulers and priests, united in mind and heart in this request, while they offer their official prayer and worship to God with sacrifices and holocausts. This type of prayer has great power with God. The early Church experienced notable manifestations of God's presence and power when they prayed as one body, one in mind and heart (see Acts 4:24–32, 12:5–19). In Matthew 18:19–20 Jesus made us a solemn promise: ". . . if two of you on earth agree to ask anything at all, it will be granted to you by my Father in heaven. For where two or three are gathered in my name, I shall be there with them." This is the power of just two or three meeting together, one in mind and heart: the power of the whole Body of Christ meeting in this way cannot be expressed. The tragedy is that so few trust the Lord, and even fewer put this to the test, so we have a world of greed and violence when it could be held in peace by the believers at prayer.

What makes collective prayer so efficacious before God is the fact that Jesus promised to be present Himself. It is a meeting of the whole Christ, head and members, and the prayer goes to the Father by the one mediator between God and man, Jesus Himself. I doubt if He made this promise to cover prayers offered for selfish reasons or self-interest.

Intercession, whether on an individual or group level, must be based on an unshakeable trust in God, in His goodness, His mercy and His fidelity to His promises. Coupled with this must be a commitment to continuous conversion, so that our lives conform to the will of God in every detail (see 2 Chronicles 7:14, Jeremiah 29:13, Mark 11:24, James 5:16, 1 John 3:22). The present psalm illustrates this, for we see the congregation offer to God sin-offerings and holocausts as they pray in deep faith and remind God of His "duty" to protect His Anointed One.

Finally, intercession is most powerful when God's people stop relying on the world for answers, and when they give up self-reliance to throw themselves fully on God's mercy and wisdom. This brings an answer to the problem on hand as we remove the obstacles to God's intervention, thus allowing Him to manifest His power to save. In other words, when we remove all worldly thinking, and all selfish motives, we experience God at His creative best, and all things are made new.

8

Psalm 21:
Celebrating the Victory

O Lord, your strength gives joy to the king;
how your saving help makes him glad!
You have granted him his heart's desire;
you have not refused the prayer of his lips.

You came to meet him with the blessings of success,
you have set on his head a crown of pure gold.
He asked you for life and this you have given,
days that will last from age to age.

Your saving help has given him glory,
You have laid upon him majesty and splendour,
you have granted your blessings to him for ever.
You have made him rejoice with the joy of your presence.

The king has put his trust in the Lord:
through the mercy of the Most High he shall stand firm.
His hand will seek and find all his foes,
his right hand find out those who hate him.

You will burn them like a blazing furnace
on the day when you appear.
And the Lord shall destroy them in his anger;
fire will swallow them up.

You will wipe out their race from the earth
and their children from the sons of men.
Though they plan evil against you,
though they plot, they shall not prevail.

For you will force them to retreat;
at them you will aim with your bow.
O Lord, arise in your strength;
we shall sing and praise your power

(vv. 1–13).

The people return to the sanctuary to praise God for David's victory, and the king is with them. As a body they render thanks to God for His mercies to them, for God has heard their prayer and granted David his heart's desire. Now victorious over all his enemies, and undisputed ruler in the land, he has received from Nathan the Prophet a promise from God that his dynasty would last for ever (see 2 Samuel 7:6–16). David acknowledges that all his honour and glory come from God; he is not slow in giving thanks. Although he is a great and powerful king, he looks upon himself as the servant of a greater king, namely God Himself.

Because he is the Lord's anointed, King David considers his own enemies as God's enemies, so he trusts that God will unmask all of them and wipe them out. God is described here as a king who behaves as rulers did in David's time. They would not allow their enemy or his descendants to survive. With God on his side David knows that the plotting of his enemies is futile.

The psalm finishes with a rousing call to God the King to arise and manifest His power, so that His friends and subjects can rejoice in His wonderful reign on the earth.

Seen here on the historical level, the psalm is very limited in scope. It exaggerates both the power and importance of the Judean kings. If, however, David is seen as a type of the Messiah, pointing to one who was greater than himself, one who would indeed deserve the title of a great king over all the earth; if what is said of David is read as a prophecy concerning the Messiah, then the psalm contains no exaggerations, but instead carries an important vision concerning the ministry of the Messiah.

On this level we see the New Covenant people look back to the victory of Jesus, the Messiah, in the Resurrection. We give thanks to God, for we are an Easter people and thanksgiving is our song. With one mind, heart and voice the body of Christ declares her joy in the manifestation of God's power on Calvary (v. 1). Yes, God the Father did grant the heart's desire of His beloved son, Jesus, and because of this redemption is now available to everyone. ". . . God shows no partiality. Rather, the man of any nation who fears God and acts uprightly is acceptable to him . . ." (Acts 10:34b, 35; N.A.B.) (v. 2). Jesus is now declared to be King of Kings and Lord of Lords, and is crowned with many crowns (v. 3) (see Revelation 14:14, 19:12, Philippians 2:10–11). In His intercession for the world Jesus had requested His Father to allow Him to give eternal life to anyone He chose (see John 5:21, 17:2, 24). His request was granted. Now, because of Him, we shall live for ever with God if we accept the gift of salvation that He won for us (v. 4). Jesus, now in glory, is surrounded by splendour and majesty, enjoying rest after the labour of His redeeming work.

From this point the psalm suddenly looks to the future and the ultimate triumph of Christ, when the kingdoms of this world will have become the kingdom of our Lord and of His Christ, and He shall reign for ever (see Revelation 11:15). All His enemies will eventually be unmasked and overthrown, punished with hell-fire, on the great day of His Second Coming, when all the nations will be judged (vv. 8, 9). No one will escape. The age of God's mercy in which we live will be over, and all of us will render an account of our lives.

The true enemies of God and His people are Satan and his minions, and they will be cast into the lake of fire for ever (v. 10) (see Revelation 20:10). Satan may plot as much as he will, using human beings who submit to him to help him; he will also use the powers of this world, for he is the Prince of this world (see John 14:30). In the end he will be utterly defeated, because Jesus promised that the gates of hell would never prevail against the Church (vv. 11–12) (see Matthew 16:18).

51

Let us all pray earnestly that God will continue to use His power to save His people from the Evil One, so that we can continue our paean of praise and thanksgiving to Him (v. 13).

This psalm teaches us to return to God with praise and thanksgiving for all His goodness to us. Prayer that lacks these elements is incomplete, for these are some of the highest religious emotions we can express. They show that we truly know God, and are in relationship with Him. Having come before Him to ask a favour, it reveals a very selfish heart when we do not return thanks. Jesus showed Himself hurt when only one of the ten lepers returned to thank Him for his healing (see Luke 17:11–19). When prayer is filled with sincere gratitude it shows the integrity of the heart, and the sincerity of the original request.

Thanksgiving, or rendering glory to God with the lips, but more especially with the heart, is so essential to prayer that the mere words "thank you" do not begin to express it. St Paul reveals the great sin of the pagan Roman Empire as the refusal to glorify God or render Him thanks (see Romans 1:21). He then describes the frightful state of immorality that the people sank into (see Romans 1:22–32). Unbelievers then, and now, get caught in the web of their own vices, with all the consequent suffering, until joy, praise and thanksgiving are unknown concepts to them. Thanksgiving and praise are normal to the sinner who has *found* the Saviour, and through Him also found the way out of his misery. As we progress in the spiritual life, experiencing the divine mercy and forgiveness more and more deeply, joy, praise and rendering glory to God become continuous. Now we not only are redeemed, we also *look* redeemed! For joy puts a radiant smile on the face, which is very beautiful (see 1 Corinthians 1:4, Philippians 1:3, Colossians 1:3, etc). To sum up the attitude of the early Church: one in mind and heart they praised God continuously with glad and joyful hearts; as the redeemed community of Jesus their main act of public worship was Eucharist – giving thanks.

9

Psalm 22:
The Suffering Messiah

Psalm 22 is one of the most wonderful pieces of writing in the Old Testament. It is a breath of pure prophecy. It speaks of the execution of a good man who relies on God in total trust throughout His ordeal. King David is the human author of this psalm, but there is no event in his life that would account for his composing this magnificent prayer. This time the other author, the Holy Spirit, is much more obvious. It is as if He said: "This time give Me the pen!"

The mysterious sufferer referred to here showed love so amazing, holiness so pure, patience so incredible, and wisdom so boundless, that He gives His identity away. It is the Messiah, Jesus of Nazareth Himself.

The title given to the psalm in the Bible is interesting: "The Hind of the Dawn". This refers to the theme of the psalm, which tells us that help, deliverance and joy come at day-break. The frightful ordeal of the Passion ended in the glory of the Resurrection at dawn on Easter Day.

My God, my God, why have you forsaken me?
You are far from my plea and the cry of my distress.
O my God, I call by day and you give no reply;
I call by night and I find no peace.

Yet you, O God, are holy,
enthroned on the praises of Israel.
In you our fathers put their trust;
they trusted and you set them free.
When they cried to you, they escaped.
In you they trusted and never in vain

(vv. 1–5).

As Jesus hung on the Cross in the final hours of His life, when darkness covered the earth (see Matthew 27:46, Mark 15:34), the opening words of this psalm came to His lips, as the expression of what He was enduring. We do not know if He prayed the whole psalm, but we do know that He experienced it to a much greater depth than the psalmist could have imagined.

In his sacred Passion, Jesus took our sufferings and sorrows upon Himself. He was pierced and crushed for our sins as He paid the price for our healing and peace (see Isaiah 53:4–5). St Paul says that Jesus actually "became a curse" for us (see Galatians 3:13). He therefore stood before God as *the sinner*, and endured the full punishment for sin, the most terrifying part of which was being cut off from God. This beloved son, whose whole motive in life was to do the Father's will, now suddenly finds Himself cut off from communion with the Father (see Matthew 3:17, 17:5, John 4:34, 14:31). He cried out in desperate anguish: "My God, . . . *why* have you deserted me? I am your beloved Son in whom you take all your delight!" The bewildered "Why?" is very touching. It was unthinkable that His Father, whom He addressed as "Abba, Daddy", would cut Him off, but He had! This is not a reproach levelled against God. It is the reaction born of shock and dismay. Now He feels that His cries of distress and His anguished prayer for help and deliverance will be lost, for there is no one to hear Him. Yet this does not stop Him. He continues to pray day and night, even though He can find no peace or rest (v. 1).

God keeps silence. Jesus turns to Him in great reverence now, addressing Him as the "Holy One of Israel". In great humility He reminds God that the Scriptures, God's own words, are full of examples of how his ancestors put their trust in God and were delivered. There was that great deliverance from Egypt under Moses, for example. There were many stories of God hearing David's prayers for help, and was He not in the line of succession from David? For this reason, is He not justified in expecting deliverance when He, too, puts His trust in God, the One who makes His presence felt in the praise and worship of His people?

The strong emphasis on trust is very important, for trust is the basis of our relationship with God. We trust His integrity, His faithfulness, His love, His word and thus find we can respond to Him. If God is not trustworthy, then all hope is gone. When this verse is read as one piece there is a strong inference written between the lines:

they trusted – you set them free
they cried – and they escaped
they trusted – and never in vain.

The hidden complaint of the sufferer is this: "Am I the only one who can genuinely trust you – in vain?" The "why" of the first line comes back strongly here, emphasizing the distress. The bewilderment lies in the fact that He is doing all He has been taught, all that the Scripture says, all that He knows to be right, but it does not seem to work for Him! His grief goes much deeper now.

> But I am a worm and no man,
> the butt of men, laughing-stock of the people.
> All who see me deride me.
> They curl their lips, they toss their heads.
> "He trusted in the Lord, let him save him;
> let him release him if this is his friend."
>
> Yes, it was you who took me from the womb,
> entrusted me to my mother's breast.
> To you I was committed from my birth,
> from my mother's womb you have been my God.
> Do not leave me alone in my distress;
> come close, there is none else to help
>
> (vv. 6–11).

In the first movement of the psalm the sufferer had looked away from Himself, upwards and outwards to God, seeking deliverance. Here in this second movement, in utter anguish, He looks at His own miserable condition and realizes that His torturers have reduced Him to the level of an earthworm. Isaiah had prophesied concerning His Passion: ". . . so disfigured did He look that He seemed no longer human . . . without beauty, without majesty . . . a thing despised and rejected by men, a man of sorrows and familiar with suffering . . ." (see Isaiah 52:14, 53:2–3; J.B.). He describes Himself now as utterly degraded and shamed before everyone, the butt of their cynical jokes. Yet the torturers were not satisfied, for they heaped scorn and mockery upon Him, as if there was no end to their desire to cause the greatest pain. They touch upon the deepest inner wound now, namely, His distress at the absence and silence of His Father. They scornfully remind Him that if He were indeed God's friend God would deliver Him, for they all knew that God was on the side of the innocent, and the oppressed (see Psalm 34:15–20, Wisdom 2:18).

Their idea of what deliverance would mean differed greatly from what God had in mind for this humble sufferer. It is a dreadful instinct in mankind that seeks to crush the poor and the suffering, to increase their pain instead of alleviating it. St Matthew 27:33–44 clearly states that this part of the psalm was fulfilled literally in Jesus on the Cross. He was jeered by the passers-by who had nothing to do with His death: He was mocked by the chief priests, scribes and elders, and taunted even by the robber who died along with Him. They laughed at Him because he had saved others but could not save Himself. They promised to believe if He would come down from the Cross in a spectacular gesture. The worst sting of all was their mockery of Him for saying that He was God's Son.

The Passion was not the first time we see Jesus of Nazareth rejected and despised by others. No. It was His daily bread throughout His life. The scribes and pharisees despised Him as a poor country rabbi with no proper education. He came from Galilee, which did not have a reputation for producing prophets. His relatives were poor, His close disciples were mere fishermen. Only the lower classes followed Him – the poor, the sick, the possessed, the despised tax-collectors, and the outcasts. The leaders, intellectuals and upper classes would have nothing to do with Him (except for a few individuals), but they were jealous of His popularity and His power.

He had been mocked before too. Scattered throughout the gospels we find that the scribes and pharisees had accused Him of being a sabbath-breaker, the worst sin of all in their eyes, apart from His claim to be the Son of God. On different occasions they called Him a glutton, a wine-bibber, a drunkard, a false prophet, an enemy of Caesar, and also of being in league with the devil. They killed Him for blasphemy, because He said He was God's Son (see Mark 2:24, Luke 7:34, 11:15, John 8:52, 19:20).

The third movement of the psalm sees the sufferer make a review of His lifelong relationship with God in faith and trust. He had been utterly dependent on God as a babe in the womb, yet God saw Him safely through birth. From the dawn of His life He has known God deeply: "You have been my very own God." Now in His hour of trouble He continues that trust in God, even when it appears to bring no results. God is the only person He can turn to, and the only one who can help.

Many bulls have surrounded me,
fierce bulls of Bashan close me in.
Against me they open wide their jaws,
like lions, rending and roaring.

Like water I am poured out,
disjointed are all my bones.
My heart has become like wax,
it is melted within my breast.
Parched as burnt clay is my throat,
my tongue cleaves to my jaws.

Many dogs have surrounded me,
a band of the wicked beset me.
They tear holes in my hands and feet
and lay me in the dust of death.

I can count every one of my bones.
These people stare at me and gloat;
they divide my clothing among them.
They cast lots for my robe

(vv. 12–18).

In this fourth movement of the psalm the sufferer looks out at those who stand around the Cross. How did He feel about them? There were several groups of people there: first there was His mother, Mary, with St John comforting her in this terrible grief. What pain it must have cost Him to see His mother so distressed. Mary of Magdala was there too, close to her saviour, and unafraid of the consequences. He was dying as a public criminal, but she knew who He was, and wanted to comfort Him by her loving presence. The chief priests, scribes and pharisees were there too, glaring and gloating at His shame, apparently enjoying His humiliation. And there were the Roman soldiers playing dice to while away the time as they waited for the men to die, even casting lots for His clothes as if He were already dead. The passers-by formed another group who got involved just out of curiosity. Finally, away in the background were all the women disciples of Jesus, and hopefully the men also!

The scene described here has often been re-enacted through the course of history; it is the strong closing in on the weak, the many on the one. The crowd is described in powerful animal images, showing the helpless fear of the dying victim in the face of all these people, whether friend or foe. The strong bulls of Bashan were known for their ferocity and fury, while dogs hunted in packs and were very fierce, and the lions hacked their prey to pieces. These powerful images describe the torture experienced in this violent death. He feels as if He is being torn asunder from within too; there was the drying up of the body fluids which was one of the results of a crucifixion. The pain caused by this was so great that it even moved the Roman soldier to show compassion by offering Jesus a drink of vinegar, which was probably the sour drink the soldiers had for themselves (see John 19:28). He was nailed to the Cross now with holes in His hands and feet, and just left there in the heat and the dust to die. Death was the only relief He could look forward to now, but God is still silent and absent. It is hell to be rejected both by God and man and this is His lot.

He looks down at His body, so wounded and diminished that He can count all His bones. He is fading away to death, yet His enemies continue to stare at Him and gloat, increasing His sense of shame and exposure. He sees the soldiers cast lots for His clothes too.

> O Lord, do not leave me alone,
> my strength, make haste to help me!
> Rescue my soul from the sword,
> my life from the grip of these dogs.
> Save my life from the jaws of these lions,
> my poor soul from the horns of these oxen
> (vv. 19–21).

In a rising crescendo the sufferer uses all the strength left to Him, and cries out across the darkness and the chasm that separates Him from God and begs for deliverance. Then in a whisper of amazement He realizes that He has been heard. God has answered Him. Following the Hebrew, the last two lines should read: "Save my life from the jaws of these lions, and from the horns of these oxen. You have answered!" It is this response from God, now manifesting His presence to the poor sufferer, which explains the second half of the psalm, both a hymn of thanksgiving and a prophecy about the future Kingdom of God.

> I will tell of your name to my brethren
> and praise you where they are assembled.
> "You who fear the Lord give him praise;
> all sons of Jacob, give him glory.
> Revere him, Israel's sons.
>
> For he has never despised
> nor scorned the poverty of the poor.
> From him he has not hidden his face,
> but he heard the poor man when he cried"
>
> (vv. 22–24).

The second half of this psalm relates to the resurrection. The holocaust has been accepted by God. These verses show that the final moments of Jesus on the Cross were in triumph, as He cried out to everyone that the redemption was now accomplished, and He could see, in prophetic vision, what lay in the future. Because of this the new community who were His Brethren would give praise and glory to God in all their assemblies. They would glorify God particularly for accepting Jesus in the humble poverty of His incarnation into a sinful world, and His poverty on the Cross when He went before God bereft of all His privileges as the beloved son, identified with all sinners so that He could save them. As Isaiah said: ". . . for allowing Himself to be taken for a sinner—" (Isaiah 53:12).

> You are my praise in the great assembly.
> My vows I will pay before those who fear him.
> The poor shall eat and shall have their fill.
> They shall praise the Lord, those who seek him.
> May their hearts live for ever and ever!

All the earth shall remember and return to the Lord,
all families of the nations worship before him
for the kingdom is the Lord's; he is ruler of the
    nations.
They shall worship him, all the mighty of the earth;
before him shall bow all who go down to the dust.

And my soul shall live for him, my children serve
    him.
They shall tell of the Lord to generations yet to
    come,
declare his faithfulness to peoples yet unborn:
"These things the Lord has done"

(vv. 25–31).

In this final movement of the psalm Jesus declares that God His Father is the theme of all praise and worship in the Church. Here the poor, who are those who rely on God for everything, spiritual and natural, just as Jesus did, will be fed by God Himself on His Word and on the Eucharist by the power of His Spirit. All may feed on Him as much as they want and give praise to God.

Suddenly the psalm peers into the distant future when all things will have been renewed, when all nations will return to God. Then we come to the *consumatus est* of the Old Testament. Jesus declared His trust in the young Church that was to suffer so much after His departure. His disciples would pick up the challenge and go, eventually, to the whole world to preach the Gospel. The generations yet unborn can be guaranteed to hear the Good News. Now it is all over (see John 19:30). He bows His head, and in dying He conquers death, taking its sting away by His redeeming blood. With St Paul we too cry out with joy: "O death where is your victory? Death where is your sting? Now the sting of death is sin – so let us thank God for giving us the victory through our Lord Jesus Christ" (see 1 Corinthians 15:55).

This psalm teaches us the important attitudes we need in

prayer. First there is humility, which enables us to recognize our own sinfulness and nothingness before God's holiness. This releases us to be able truly to praise and thank Him, and to reach out in real trust. When humility has matured it enables us to trust God even when He appears to be absent from us, when we feel all alone. Childlike humility enables us quietly to trust in God's faithfulness, mercy and love (Isaiah 30:15,18). It also makes us persist in prayer. Many people give up when persistence would have got them all that they wanted. They do not realize that God wants to do more for us than we would ever ask or imagine (see Luke 11:5–8, 18:1–8, Ephesians 3:21). The childlike, humble persistence of Jesus won an eternal redemption for all of us. He did not give up when all the odds were stacked against Him. Let us learn from Him.

10

Psalm 23:
The Loving Shepherd

This most popular and best-loved of all the psalms was written by David, the "sweet singer of Israel" (see 2 Samuel 23:1). It has gained immortality by virtue of its childlike expressions, and the sweet charm of its train of thought and imagery. It expresses the serene joy of a soul that has found peace of mind and heart in its union with God. His faith matured by many trials, the poet now rests in complete trust in his Lord, whom he found utterly faithful in his time of need.

The Lord is my shepherd;
there is nothing I shall want.
Fresh and green are the pastures
where he gives me repose.
Near restful waters he leads me,
to revive my drooping spirit.

He guides me along the right path;
he is true to his name.
If I should walk in the valley of darkness
no evil would I fear.
You are there with your crook and your staff;
with these you give me comfort.

You have prepared a banquet for me
in the sight of my foes.
My head you have anointed with oil;
my cup is overflowing.

> Surely goodness and kindness shall follow me
> all the days of my life.
> In the Lord's own house shall I dwell
> for ever and ever
>
> (vv. 1–6).

To express his relationship with God David chose the very popular image of the shepherd-king. He had spent his youth as a shepherd himself, and so understood all the love, concern, compassion and selfless giving required of a shepherd. He now utilizes this knowledge to proclaim God's goodness to us. Since I have spent time in dialogue with David in this psalm, and hopefully with the Holy Spirit too, I hope that the dialogue which follows with you, the reader, will enable you to appreciate from a New Testament angle what the poet expressed in the idiom of his own day.

The whole message of the psalm is contained in the first verse: "The Lord is MY shepherd." If we grasp the implications of this statement, we shall understand all that follows, for it flows from it. In the ancient world every person was under authority to someone else. It was the *pater familias* for the family, and the elders of the town, or the local chieftain, the priests in the Temple, and over all others was the king. The opening question of the psalm is: "Who is your shepherd?" My reply may take you a little by surprise. It is the Lord God Himself: He takes personal care of me. He guides, teaches and protects me just as shepherds do their sheep. And I am privileged to enjoy His indwelling mystic presence always (see John 14:20, 23). It is because of this I declare that I am lacking in nothing, since He takes care of all my needs (see Matthew 6:11). You may ask "When did God become your shepherd?" I reply, joyfully, that He has loved me ever since my life began in my mother's womb (see Psalm 22:10, 139:13–15). He has been my unseen friend all my life, and He is my shepherd now in a living, on-going relationship of two persons interacting with each other in loving intimacy (see John 14:20, 23, 26, etc). In surprise, maybe even disbelief, you ask: "Do you mean that the great transcendent God, who revealed Himself to Moses in cloud and fire and terrible awesomeness, is relating to you, a mere nobody, in this way?" Joyfully I reply: "Yes!" Because Jesus, God's Son, came to us in the incarnation, because He died for us in order to redeem us, I can call the great God of creation, the ruler of the universe, the God of Abraham, Isaac and Jacob my Daddy. And I have claims upon Him as His redeemed adopted child. With Jesus His beloved son I have become a co-heir to His Kingdom in glory. Right now I enjoy the privileges of a member of His family (see Mark 14:36, Romans 8:15,17, 21).

You may object that the shepherd image is too lowly to express such an exalted privilege. Yet you will agree that we must use images that mean something to us. In his many years minding sheep, David learned the constant care that these fairly helpless animals needed, in a country where wild animals roamed freely, and sheep and lambs were easy prey, even for relatively small animals, and he applied that knowledge to our relationship with God. For one thing a shepherd had to live among his sheep; he had to watch over them day and night, and this for the whole of their lives, from birth to death. Therefore, each sheep was known personally and intimately. Each one was called by its own name. It was never just one of a crowd. The very first lesson for the sheep was to recognize the shepherd's voice and to learn to respond *only* to that voice; as well as to recognize its own identity, and respond to its own name when the shepherd called. The shepherd had to provide both food and protection, while taking personal care of the health of his flock. In short, he took care of everything, so that the sheep could live a care-free life in a world full of danger and trouble.

Now God is all this to us and much more, so you will understand why I go on to say that I lack nothing, because

65

God's divine providence takes care of all my needs (see Matthew 6:25–34). All God asks of me is that I submit to His perfect will and plan for my life, given to me out of infinite love. The image of the sheep tells me that I am not very important of myself, and have no great value in the eyes of the world. It is God's love that clothes me with greatness. Everything I am, everything I have, whatever I shall become, comes from Him, hence my boast is not of myself: my boast is of Him. I have a great Shepherd. (See John chapter 10, where Jesus uses all these ideas to explain our relationship with Him. See also Psalm 34:2, 2 Corinthians 10:17.)

God Who sees everything, knows what is best for me. He chooses the pastureland I am to graze in. Being a stupid little sheep I would wander off anywhere I saw grass, thinking that all grass must be good. He knows differently, so He chooses the circumstances of my life very carefully, making sure that all my needs will be taken care of, and that I shall be nourished on food that leads to eternal life. Otherwise I should be in danger of being led astray, or even poisoned by false doctrines. When I stay in His pasture, I grow to full stature and reach the place of true rest for my soul. My food is to draw life from prayer, from His Word in the Holy Scriptures, and from Himself in the Eucharist. In this way I learn at the highest level of my being. I find that the more I nourish my soul, the more peace and repose I experience in the depths of my being, even though there may be trouble and turmoil on the surface of my life. To empower me to cope with the storms of life, He teaches me to drink deeply from the waters of His grace and life that flow abundantly to all thirsty souls (see John 7:37). As I learn to draw power and grace from Him in all the daily events of my life, I find that He heals and restores me at an ever deeper level of my being, so that joy overflows into every part of my life. Thus He keeps me pure and free from evil, while protecting me from the contamination of a world ruled by atheistic humanism.

Besides, I discover that in relating to Him I enter into a training programme for life, where He continuously shows me the right path to follow. There are many paths to follow in this world, and many ways to God. He reveals the right one for me. To hear His guidance I must learn to live in an attitude of listening and obedience to His will. I must allow Him to correct me when I go astray, for sheep wander off easily, allowing their attention to be caught by useless, even harmful things. They forget that they are surrounded by spiritual enemies who can injure or even destroy them. My protection lies in staying close to my shepherd, and keeping my eyes on Him, following His footsteps, and answering to His call alone.

Amazingly His reputation is at stake in this relationship. When others look at me and see a healthy, well-nourished sheep which is growing to its full potential, they will say that He is a good shepherd. But the reverse is also true: if they observe me sickly, weak and miserable they will say that He is a bad shepherd. In a very real sense I am His advertisement to the unbelieving world. He not only wants me redeemed but looking and acting redeemed! (see Romans 2:24). I have a responsibility to respond to His grace offered to me.

Fully surrendered to His will now, and to His guidance, I do not fret or worry over those difficult times in life which otherwise might drag me down into depression, or even breakdown. Neither do I fear the changes of life or the onset of old age and death, because in all these events I am protected by the shepherd's crook and staff. The crook is a short cudgel which He uses to defend me against enemy attacks, be they fear, anxiety, depression or anything else. I run to Him who is my shield, my defence, my protector, and I am unafraid. His staff is His walking stick, which He frequently uses on the sheep to discipline them; in this way He brings me back when I wander off in anger, rebellion or unbelief from His perfect will for my life. Between that crook and staff I know that I am safe from any foe, either inside or outside myself. You will see, therefore, that He is a great shepherd.

Not only am I unafraid of trials ahead or any lurking danger from enemies, but I am so secure in His love that He allows me, even during this earthly pilgrimage, to feast at His table, the table of His Word, the table of the Eucharist, and the Table of His own heart (see John 13:25). I know that this is a foretaste of the messianic banquet in Heaven. What a joy for me, a poor sinner! Can you see now why I said that if you understood the meaning of "the Lord is my shepherd" you would grasp everything else?

His love is so great that He gives me even more gifts, with the anointing of His Holy Spirit, and with the oil of salvation. Now my cup of joy brims over. Gratitude knows no bounds in my heart; it just bubbles up like a heavenly champagne!

My expectation for the future, under such a loving Master, is bright indeed, for I shall experience His loving kindness and His infinite goodness all of my days. I also look forward to the heavenly mansion He has prepared for me when my pilgrimage on earth is over. There I shall rejoice in His presence always. Because the Lord is my shepherd I lack nothing good in this life or the next. If only our poor grief-stricken world could hear this good news! Then they, too, could hear His voice, and follow my shepherd to green pastures until there is but one fold and one shepherd (John 10, 14:2).

11

Psalm 27:
The Conquest of Fear

This psalm is considered by some scholars to be two
separate psalms pieced together at a date later than its
composition by King David. They maintain that vv. 1–6
form a song of confidence, while vv. 7–14 are a lament. Yet
it is possible to view the psalm as a unity. It is presented that
way in the Psalter, and we shall treat it as such. The
historical background of the psalm is very difficult to
discover, and various theories have been put forward. This
psalm describes the experience of David, who seeks refuge
in the presence of God while he is still at a distance from the
sanctuary and surrounded by enemies. He sings of his
unshakeable confidence in God. As he approaches the
sanctuary he pours out his heart to God in sorrow, while he
maintains his stance of deep faith.

The Lord is my light and my help;
whom shall I fear?
The Lord is the stronghold of my life;
before whom shall I shrink?

When evil-doers draw near
to devour my flesh,
it is they, my enemies and foes,
who stumble and fall.

Though an army encamp against me
my heart would not fear.
Though war break out against me
even then would I trust.

There is one thing I ask of the Lord,
for this I long,
to live in the house of the Lord,
all the days of my life,
to savour the sweetness of the Lord,
to behold his temple.

For there he keeps me safe in his tent
in the day of evil.
He hides me in the shelter of his tent,
on a rock he sets me safe.

And now my head shall be raised
above my foes who surround me
and I shall offer within his tent
a sacrifice of joy.

I will sing and make music for the Lord
(vv. 1–6).

The triumphant faith expressed in these lovely verses owes nothing to the exuberance of youth, or to the refusal of the adult to face the seriousness of the situation on hand. Instead, it manifests the maturity of one who is grounded in a faith and trust that has developed through many trials. Inwardly fortified by his strong vibrant faith, David can now "lift up his head" in confidence and hope among the present pressing problems.

Like Psalm 23 this song declares its entire message in the first verse: "the Lord is my light and my help (salvation), whom shall I fear?" These words, so full of power and joy, proclaim David's stance before God. His personal experience of prayer has taught David that God has been his salvation and deliverance in every difficulty brought to Him. God is on his side, so why should he fear a human foe? (see Romans 8:31). Yet this prayer of his shows that he experiences the normal fears we all go through; but he seeks to overcome them by his trust in God. Like us, he is utterly dependent on God for everything; he finds that his calm trust in God frees him from fear and anxiety, enabling God to act on his behalf (see John 11:39). This grace is only experienced by those who are utterly given to God, those for whom God is their ultimate goal in the actual practical circumstances of everyday life. It is right here that one finds the deepest roots of a heroic attitude to life. David calls God his *light*, the ultimate source of all that is good, and of all joy. God is also the source of his inner strength, the One who protects and fortifies him for the daily struggle (v. 1).

The certitude of his faith and the strength he draws from it enables David to face his enemies and oppressors without fear, no matter how fierce they are. Even if they come against him in great numbers, surrounding him on all sides, it cannot shake the inward calm and assurance that comes from his trust in God. His position is clear: "Be still and know that I am God." He is allowing God to *be* God, so he does not allow himself the luxury of anxiety or fear. His heart remains in unruffled calm and peace, for he knows what the ultimate fate of the evil-doers will be. God is the Lord of hosts, and to Him alone belongs ultimate power. Because of this the psalmist need no longer linger over his own puny affairs, but can centre his attention on God alone. With his thoughts focused completely on God, he is now able to make wise decisions, for his faith has gained that inner balance and confident strength he needed. The words of Isaiah hold good for him now: "the believer shall not stumble" (see Isaiah 28:16; J.B.) (vv. 2–3).

The poet now reveals the source of his great courage and inward strength. It emanates from a tender childlike relationship with God, which finds expression in the succeeding verses. The deepest desire of his heart is to live in perpetual communion with God. If he can reach this, he has everything he wants. It is not that he wishes to live continuously in the sanctuary – this would be impossible – but the sanctuary represents the concrete experience of nearness to God. He wishes to become a member of God's household, and to be privileged to walk with God all the days of his life, just as the saints did of old (see Genesis 17:1, etc). Jesus answered this prayer by making all of us members of God's household by our adoption, and sharing with us His own privileges as the Son of God (see Ephesians 2:19–22, John 17:24).

It would be wrong to restrict the closeness to God with the sanctuary, the Temple, or even the formal times of worship. The personal relationship with God is continuous; it merely finds its expression in the formal liturgy. The outward ceremonies of the liturgy, devoid of this inner content, can become meaningless ritual. This is the great temptation of an organized worship. God wants us to worship Him "in spirit and in truth" (see John 4:23). This demands the inner content that enables us to worship God with our whole lives, and be constantly in touch with Him as the source of all our good. It is a shame to limit this to the formal times of worship.

"To behold the sweetness of the Lord" means the ability to relish God's goodness, beauty and majesty; to be captivated by His attractive loveliness. Once people have really tasted this, they will long to have it, as David does here, on a permanent basis. It is in this continuing intimacy with God that we are cured of our worldly attitudes, and given the ability to see and pray from the stance of faith and trust in God (v. 4).

This communion with God is the safe tent and the secure refuge in difficult times. God is the everlasting rock on which our lives are built in safety. We can trust God completely (v. 5). Since David's heart is assured of victory through faith, he can lift up his head now and offer God a sacrifice of joy and thanksgiving, thus surrendering his whole being to God, who is the object of all his happiness. We see here a real communion with God, a mutual giving and receiving. The joy and strength that flow from it can be compared to an overflowing fountain, because the little ego has been conquered, and the glory of God can flow from this man's life (v. 6). Jesus promised this overflowing abundance of joy and peace to anyone who would come to Him for life. He also said that we would know the continual presence of the Holy Spirit as our sanctifier and teacher, whose anointing would enable us to overcome all obstacles and even do the same works as Jesus did Himself (see John 7:37, 14:12, 16, 17, 26, 27, 15:11, 16).

O Lord, hear my voice when I call;
have mercy and answer.
Of you my heart has spoken:
"Seek his face."

It is your face, O Lord, that I seek;
hide not your face.
Dismiss not your servant in anger;
you have been my help.

Do not abandon or forsake me,
O God my help!
Though father and mother forsake me,
the Lord will receive me.

Instruct me, Lord, in your way;
on an even path lead me.
When they lie in ambush protect me
from my enemy's greed.
False witnesses rise against me,
breathing out fury.

I am sure I shall see the Lord's goodness
in the land of the living.
Hope in him, hold firm and take heart.
Hope in the Lord!

(vv. 7–14).

In these verses, David, very conscious of the dangers surrounding him, cries to God for help, clinging to Him as his only source of hope. He appeals to God's merciful love for an answer to his troubles, while reminding himself of his need to seek God in order to surrender to Him and His will (v. 7). He is seeking God now, and he begs to be heard – in the sense that his case will be dealt with. Otherwise he feels he will be dismissed like a servant (see Amos 5:4, Jeremiah 29:12ff). Because God has been so good to him in the past he begs for a favourable hearing now. The problem is that if God does not hear his prayer, there is no help for him anywhere.

David wrestles in prayer between God's just judgement on his sinfulness, and God's mercy and fidelity to His promises. It is precisely here that the tension of living by faith lies. We know that if God abandons us, we deserve it, but He never abandons those who cling to His mercy and love! Hence David declares that even if his own parents deserted him, God would not. He is God's child, and a child who chooses to relate to God as Father, rather than experience Him as judge. We see this principle in the gospel where Jesus responded to people as they presented themselves. The outcasts and sinners who were not ashamed to repent and seek His forgiveness, found Jesus to be the mercy and love of God incarnate, but the pharisees, and others who were unwilling to change, found in Jesus a just and terrible judge; for when He uncovered their sins, He did so in public, and with deadly accuracy and truth (see Matthew 23:13–36). The tragedy in both Testaments is that there was no necessity to relate to God as a judge when He offered Himself as mercy and love in redemption (v. 10).

Aware now of human weakness, and its terrifying ability to fall back into error and sinfulness, David begs God to teach him the right way, God's way to live. The pressure of trouble all around him makes it more urgent for him to seek God more deeply, and having done so, he now confidently asks for protection. Only those who have surrendered their hearts humbly to the will of God, and are ready to act in obedience to it, will avoid the trap of making God into a servant of their own desires, in asking for external help. Thus the psalmist's petitions do not take the form of begging; they have become true prayer (vv. 11–12).

David has regained his inward and outward peace through prayer, and speaks now of the strength of his faith. He knows that he can have communion with God and experience God's goodness during his lifetime. The daily encounter with God in prayer will ensure this, and God will become, increasingly, his support and strength. We can see here that a deep, living faith enables us to cope with the trials and tribulations of life; it will drive us into the arms of God to receive an increasing supply of the mercy, forgiveness and strength which give us the supernatural ability to cope with suffering and sorrow.

This wonderful psalm expresses the experience of a person committed to God in a deep and sustained prayer-life. I doubt if it would express the experience of one whose prayer-life was spasmodic. Prayer is that deep well from which all must drink if they would grow in faith and trust towards God. It is a very mature faith, one that has been tried and tested, one that can say, in deep peace, that it fears no enemy, either from within (our spiritual enemies) or from without. It manifests itself in complete freedom from anxiety, and in the courage to rest in God and let Him work out the details of our lives. Very few can rest peacefully when everyone turns against them, for it demands the surrender of the heart to God, with all its desires and affections. Yet we are not safe unless protected by this love relationship, through which God's will is being carried out in our lives. Hidden in the safety of the heart of Jesus our lives are built on the rock.

Nevertheless we cannot sit back saying that "we have made it". We need to continue to seek God more deeply each day, as we grow in the knowledge of our own sinfulness and of His boundless mercy. Relating to God as

Father and Saviour gives us the correct blend that releases His loving mercy and protectiveness towards us. Thus we can be sure of continuing our life of loving union with Him, leaving us in the position of proclaiming to others our hope in God.

12

Psalm 30:
Mourning into Dancing

This psalm, written by David, is given a secondary title in the Bible: "Canticle for the dedication of the house". As the title suggests, the psalm was written for either the dedication of David's own palace in Jerusalem (see 2 Samuel 5:11), or for the dedication of the sanctuary, for the Temple was not built in David's time. It may also mean, and many scholars think that it does, that the psalm was later adapted for use on the Feast of Hanukkah, the Feast of the dedication of the Temple which was instituted by Judas Maccabeus in 165 BC, to commemorate the restoration of the Temple that year.

Without this secondary title the psalm would seem to be a thanksgiving song to God after a severe illness. If indeed it was used for the Hanukkah feast then it was re-interpreted so that the deliverance of the individual, in vv. 2–8, came to be understood as the deliverance of the nation from the persecution of Antiochus Epiphanes. This is an important point because it illustrates that down the centuries the psalms have been re-interpreted for each generation, so that the enduring message of the psalm could be read in the new situation, and new peoples could receive guidance and hope from them. It is important that we truly hear these inspired prayers interpret our own spiritual lives for us.

> I will praise you, Lord, you have rescued me
> and have not let my enemies rejoice over me.

O Lord, I cried to you for help
and you, my God, have healed me.
O Lord, you have raised my soul from the dead,
restored me to life from those who sink into the grave.

Sing psalms to the Lord, you who love him,
give thanks to his holy name.
His anger lasts but a moment; his favour through life.
At night there are tears, but joy comes with dawn.

I said to myself in my good fortune:
"Nothing will ever disturb me."
Your favour has set me on a mountain fastness,
then you hid your face and I was put to confusion.

To you, Lord, I cried,
to my God I made appeal:
"What profit would my death be, my going to the grave?
Can dust give you praise or proclaim your truth?"

The Lord listened and had pity.
The Lord came to my help.
For me you have changed my mourning into dancing,
you removed my sackcloth and girdled me with joy.
So my soul sings psalms to you unceasingly.
O Lord my God, I will thank you for ever

(vv. 1–12).

The psalmist begins with a burst of praise and thanks to
God for his deliverance from death. He feels that he has
been hauled up from the pit of death, like a bucket from a
cistern, or a prisoner from a dungeon (see Jeremiah 38:10).
He had, obviously, put his faith and trust in God, so his
deliverance is a triumph for faith also. If the ever present
enemies had got the upper hand in his death, it would be a
shattering blow to his faith (v. 1). He now realizes how
closely his life depended on God's mercy and loving-

kindness. God has healed him, so he now accepts life as a gift from God, with gratitude. Besides, death would have been a grim affair for him. David did not have our revelation of eternal life with God after death, and he felt that death somehow cut him off from contact with God. But now, with the gift of life given back to him, he can see things from God's perspective. Some of the attitudes he formerly held must go in consequence (vv. 2–3).

Just as the psalmist called initially upon himself to praise God, so now he enjoins the community of God's people to do the same, especially if they truly love God, for what he has experienced as an individual is also true for the community of faith. The whole psalm bears testimony to this (v. 4). He declares that the anger or wrath of God lasts but a moment, while His favour remains for life. He is not trivializing the wrath of God here, but saying that since it is the wrath of God, it springs from a different source from the anger of human beings (see Hosea 11:8).

God has placed us in a moral universe which operates on inexorable laws which we break to our own destruction. For example, if we work against the laws of agriculture we destroy the harvest; if we break the laws of architecture we destroy buildings, with loss of life; if we break the laws of health which govern our bodies, we destroy our lives; if we interfere with our environment, we can wipe out life from the planet. The suffering entailed because of this, is spoken of in the Bible as the wrath of God. It is meant to be an instrument of God's grace given to us for repentance: it is not intended merely for destruction, as the anger of man often is. The wrath of God is also given for our instruction in the ways of God. As we begin to open up and learn from it, we experience God's mercy and forgiveness, and we are healed. Thus God makes everything turn out for the good for those who turn to Him in sincerity (see Romans 8:28, 2 Corinthians 4:17–18). The pain that the Lord permits us to suffer as we slowly learn to walk in His ways is not worth talking about, when we compare it with the weight of glory that He is offering to anyone who will accept His guidance and His redeeming grace. This is why David breaks out again to proclaim the triumph of God's grace over all the events of life. There is always another day, a fresh start, a resurrection after death. God's grace and power can accomplish anything, so the psalmist overflows with joy and gratitude (v. 5).

Looking back, the psalmist realizes that he did not always have his present humble joy. Instead, he had the self-complacency and self-confidence of one who had not been tried and tested. Only now does he see that he was relying upon himself, and not at all upon God. It took the heavy trial he has just come through, to bring him to rely upon God in a real way. It is a salutary revelation to discover that one has been seeking the self, with its many goals and demands, when one should have been seeking God's will, which alone can give proper direction to one's life. While proclaiming ourselves religious we were, in fact, on an ego trip. It is sheer grace and mercy on God's part to disillusion us about this, and to enable us to face reality as it really is, in ourselves. This opens the door to growth and new life. Our lives are in fact utterly dependent on God, so it is sheer folly to rely on self, which only puts off the day of grace.

David did not face the truth until God hid His face from him, until God withdrew His favour. The bed of suffering brought him to his senses, as it does with so many of us, and it made him search his own soul. He then recognized the hand of God in his pain, which required of him to desist from the self-assurance that was leading him astray. Now he finds himself afflicted, both externally in his sickness, and internally in the confusion and lostness of his soul. He is thrown into a real crisis that opens his eyes to recognize the grace God is offering in the very withdrawal of His favour. It was this combination of the wrath of God with the saving grace offered to him that released this man from the death of soul and body. It was a veritable resurrection!

Whereas it would have been a tragedy to be released in body but remain dead in sin (vv. 6–7).

The Scriptures tell us that God only acts out of love, so it is important for us to see the wrath of God in this light also. Whatever God allows to befall us, if we turn to Him it will become a means of salvation for us. And we must not limit Him just to healing our bodies, which we must eventually leave behind us in death. This would be to short-change His gift of salvation, which includes the whole person. Jesus illustrated this principle in the healing of the paralytic. He had been asked only to heal the body, but He began with the healing of the soul. The body was also healed; but the primary healing is that of the inner man, and this healing affects everything else in life, and can even cause the outward healing of the body (see Psalm 145:17, Mark 2:1–12).

David had prayed fervently to God for his life, because he had seen where he was wrong. This is exactly what God wants us to do when we experience His wrath, or any kind of sorrow. David reasoned that his healing would release him to praise God, whereas his death at this point would accomplish nothing, either for God's glory or his own salvation (vv. 9–10).

The Lord saw that the motives of David's heart were sincere, so He responded with His healing grace. The result was that David committed himself to God in humble trust, and his heart was changed – the more important healing. His gratitude overflows to God now. The sorrow and mourning have been transformed to dancing and joy. He realizes, too, that his life has been given back to him so that he can testify to others who need a similar transformation (vv. 11–13).

This psalm celebrates one of the greatest enlightenments along the spiritual journey. Most beginners in prayer are unaware of their motivation, both in seeking God and in the service of their neighbour. So often they seek themselves in God, for they must enjoy prayer, and feel peace, and be able to report significant experiences in prayer. They confuse their own enthusiasm with religious fervour, and deceive themselves that they are truly relying on God in faith and trust, whereas, in fact, they are relying on their own health, strength, vigour and freshness in the spiritual journey. This has a very blinding effect, and they can become real Pharisees without realizing it. They fast twice a week, pay tithes, attend prayer meetings and many religious functions – all of which makes them feel better than their fellow beings, who are worldly in their ways. Moreover, they do not realize that their propensity to criticize and condemn others, their fault-finding, is equally worldly, unloving and unspiritual!

Nevertheless, God sees the heart, and behind all our faults there is often a sincere desire to seek God. So in mercy, and in response to our prayer for a deeper union with Him, God may allow sickness or tragedy to befall us, while at the same time keeping a distance from us in prayer. We appear to have lost everything in one fell swoop! The result of this is often that our world falls apart, and many of our theories and tidy doctrines go with it – those neat explanations and "answers" that we offered to others in their need, but which do not stand up to a real test. They are seen now to be hollow, for they were not born in the furnace of suffering.

Dazed and confused we go seeking God differently now. Using no religious clichés to hid our emptiness, we just cry out to God in loneliness, darkness, maybe even despair. God would achieve nothing from the death or destruction of our spiritual lives – we know that. Yet this is what seems to be the inevitable result of this trial, which came both from our own stupidity and sinfulness; as inevitable as the hand of God stretched out to save us. If we have the wisdom to reach out to grasp that hand, which appears only to punish us, we will find to our astonishment that we meet a loving Saviour. He wants to use this suffering to open our eyes to new self-knowledge, which is essential to growth.

Our personal history is, like the history of mankind as a whole, made up of a combination of God's action in our lives and our response to it. God uses the ordinary stuff of daily living to sanctify us, but we must be willing to let Him teach us. Then we discover that whether particular circumstances came about through our own fault or not, He will use them for our sanctification if we are open to learn. How good God is!

With repentance, a deep joy breaks out in us, for we now know by experience what before we knew only by hearsay. The result is spontaneous praise, and a desire to share the testimony of God's goodness with others, so that they, too, will know this joy, becoming open to this interior grace of enlightenment, which will speed them on the road to the final liberation from the self. Only those who have thrown off the sackcloth of the domination of the self can really dance for joy.

Perhaps we can now appreciate the sheer joy and delight of Mary of Magdala on Easter Day, when she heard her beloved Jesus call her by name in the midst of her mourning in the garden. Turning around, she threw herself at His feet and clung to her beloved master in ecstatic joy. Surely that lovely Jewish lady, for whom the Psalter was a daily prayer book, remembered the final words of this psalm which found wonderful fulfilment in her at that moment: "The Lord came to my help. For me you have changed my mourning into dancing, you removed my sackcloth and girdled me with joy. O Lord my God, I will thank you for ever."

An Easter Church is one that has passed through the crucible of suffering, and has gone on to the joy of the victory of Christ, in living the resurrection in its daily pilgrimage. It is one that is empowered by the coming of the Spirit at Pentecost, and therefore knows the presence of the Spirit of God in all her actions, and the power of the Spirit in her apostolate. Hence joy, praise and thanksgiving are her constant expression of prayer to God, and these sentiments are even found in her petitions.

13

Psalm 32:
The Joy of Forgiveness

Psalm 32, composed by David, is one of the seven penitential Psalms: the others are Psalms 6, 38, 51, 102, 130 and 143. It was written after the experience of sin and forgiveness, and the author looks back to learn the lessons of this. He also wants to share them with all others who are sincerely seeking to walk with God. The psalm is, therefore, a complex of thanksgiving and instruction, which accounts for its uneven style.

Happy the man whose offence is forgiven,
whose sin is remitted.
O happy the man to whom the Lord
imputes no guilt,
in whose spirit is no guile.

I kept it secret and my frame was wasted.
I groaned all the day long
for night and day your hand
was heavy upon me.
Indeed, my strength was dried up
as by the summer's heat.

But now I have acknowledged my sins;
my guilt I did not hide.
I said: "I will confess
my offence to the Lord."
And you, Lord, have forgiven
the guilt of my sin.

So let every good man pray to you
in the time of need.
The floods of water may reach high
but him they shall not reach.
You are my hiding place, O Lord;
you save me from distress.
(You surround me with cries of deliverance.)

I will instruct you and teach you
the way you should go;
I will give you counsel
with my eye upon you.

Be not like horse and mule, unintelligent,
needing bridle and bit,
else they will not approach you.
Many sorrows has the wicked
but he who trusts in the Lord,
loving mercy surrounds him.

Rejoice, rejoice in the Lord,
exult, you just!
O come, ring out your joy,
all you upright of heart

(vv. 1–11).

The psalm begins with a double beatitude which was wrung from David with his heart's blood. The sweet knowledge that he possesses now was gained through an agonizing battle which was fought out in his soul in prayer, a battle against self, but he now holds the palm of victory. Surrendered to God, he ardently desires to help others, so that they, too, will come to this happy state of mind and heart. For one who has not experienced the forgiveness of sin in this deep personal way, the emphasis on the liberating role of forgiveness may seem strange. The dreadful burden of guilt has been lifted, thus relieving the sinner from the torment of self-recrimination. Yet all that was required of him on God's part was humility and truthfulness in facing his sin and confessing it. Deceit and cover-up would prevent the very deliverance sought. What a small price to pay for peace of mind! (vv. 1–2).

In Romans 4:4–8 St Paul stresses the privilege it is for God to consider us, and therefore deal with us, as though we were righteous in His sight. This is His gift, which cannot be merited by us, but which we take hold of by faith. It is so great that it draws a response of gratitude and love from the heart of the healed sinner.

David now explains the inner struggle which preceded this grace. His simplicity and candour before God are deeply moving. He is unafraid to let God into the dark caverns of his soul, and he can help us here, for most people fear to open up deeply to God in prayer. They dread that floodlight, which will show up the murky depths and questionable motivation that lies deep within them, shut off from the intruding gaze of the world, and even from themselves. Yet salvation lies in opening these very areas to the forgiving and healing light of God. David began, like so many sinners, by trying to run away from God, pretending that he had not sinned. The basic instinct of the sinner is this flight from God, the desire to cover up, and to blame others (see Genesis 3:8–13).

Conscience was alive in David, tormenting him with guilt and shame, even causing him bodily illness. All too well do we know today that buried anger, frustration, shame, guilt, bitterness, resentment and unforgiveness – to name but a few of our problems – can cause a host of psychological and psychosomatic illnesses, which make emotional cripples out of us. These sicknesses can be controlled by drugs, but can only be healed, and the sufferer freed completely, by confession, forgiveness and inner healing. How many people waste away under the relentless pressure of a bad conscience, when release and freedom can be so easily obtained! The person concealing guilt cannot rest day or night, for peace of mind, which is the fruit of repentance, is denied them. Like the poet in "The Hound of Heaven" they say to dawn "be sudden", and to eve "be soon", for day and night are both intolerable. The nights are tortured by insomnia, and the days by pressures they have less and less ability to cope with. What weariness of soul is here, when it is all so unnecessary!

Clearly, David knows how close are the links between mind and body, and that the body reflects outwardly the inner state of the soul. More discernment is needed today to deal with the true cause of illness, so aptly termed dis-ease. Peace of mind is the opposite of dis-ease, and is a gift from God (see John 14:27). Like Francis Thompson, David feels pursued by the Hound of Heaven, but only to achieve true peace of soul in the experience of salvation (vv. 3–4).

Broken and bruised, exhausted by his stubborn resistance to grace, David finally surrendered to God. The prodigal had come home, to find new life in the forgiving embrace of a loving God and Father. The shepherd had found His stray sheep. All that was needed now was the courage and humility to let the great doctor heal the sick being (see Isaiah 1:4–6, Matthew 9:12). How can sinful man stand before the all-holy God? Only by opening up, in truth, the reality that is in his heart. God knows that we are all sinners. The moment of truth and freedom comes when we enter into this self-knowledge and then throw ourselves upon the mercy of God. Admitting sin to ourselves is not enough, we must confess candidly to God in such a manner that His merciful love can be released to us. Peace immediately floods the soul, bringing the realization that forgiveness has been granted. This, in turn, unleashes both joy and thankfulness, which are the fruits of real repentance (v. 5) – hence verses 1 and 2. It is only at this point that David realizes that the heavy hand of God upon him during the time of his stubborn resistance was, in fact, the call of God to new life, grace and glory. He can thank God for not giving up on him before the time was right. This revelation explains that the wrath of God works for the salvation of anyone who will co-operate with divine providence in their daily life. This part of the Good News is rarely appreciated.

In the sanctuary, and surrounded by the throngs of worshippers, David tells God why everyone turns to Him in times of trouble: because He allows Himself to be found by us. God always responds positively to our entreaties. Prayer is, therefore, the way to the heart of God. There you find protection from the trials of life, not as an escape from reality, but as a source of strength to deal with the realities of our trials and sorrows. To hide in the heart of God is to become clothed with power from on high, which enables us to overcome even the greatest temptations. Safe now in his new and grace-filled relationship with God, David experiences the presence of God as a strong bulwark around him. He knows, too, that God will deliver him from any and all future troubles (vv. 6–7).

In the final section of the psalm David is anxious that others learn from his bitter struggle how to stay on the road of righteousness. He counsels them from his own experience, using a parable to warn them against behaving like the stubborn mule – a good symbol of his own resistance to grace. There should be no necessity for God to have to control us in the way a horse is controlled through the bit in its mouth. This would symbolize the use of law to make us do something which should be done as a free response to God in love. God wants us to have a teachable spirit, not to persist in stubborn self-will and hardness of heart. He seeks the surrender of the heart in repentant love.

Nevertheless, it is clear that people choose differently. The wicked, who persist in their sinning, leave themselves without protection. They may even "force" God to let them experience the results of their own actions in tragedy and suffering. Having travelled this road, David is anxious to show them "The way of Peace", the right way, and he hopes that all will listen to him (see Luke 1:77–79).

The psalm concludes with David calling upon all the righteous to walk this road of peace, to exult and rejoice in the Lord, and in the salvation He offers to all repentant sinners. This Old Testament prayer is the most impressive testimony to the truth expressed by St John in his first Letter: If we say, "We are free of the guilt of sin", we deceive ourselves; the truth is not to be found in us. But if we acknowledge our sins, he who is just can be trusted to forgive our sins and cleanse us from every wrong (1 John 1:8ff; N.A.B.).

14

Psalms 42 and 43:
Struggling in Prayer

While each of this pair of psalms could be sung separately, they also constitute a single, close-knit poem, one of the most sadly beautiful in the Psalter. This is clear, not only from the early Hebrew manuscripts, which indicate no break between the psalms, but also from the fact that Psalm 43 has no title. They also reveal an identical rhythm, with the same recurring refrain (see 42:5,11, 43:5), and they have the same theme.

The author is one of the sons of Korah, and therefore a Levite, who is in exile in the north, far away from the Temple in Jerusalem which he longs for. He lives in the district which later history called Caesarea Philippi, an area where the Jordan river rushes down into the valley below from the slopes of Mount Hermon (42:6f). The sons of Korah had a chequered history. As a group of Levites they had had responsibility for the Temple worship (see 2 Chronicles 20:19), but they had been demoted. The reason why the present author was in exile is not known (see 1 Chronicles 9:31). We find him pining for the House of God, and for the intimacy he once enjoyed with God there. He feels wounded and hurt, and pours out his soul to God in this deeply moving lamentation:

> Like the deer that yearns
> for running streams,
> so my soul is yearning
> for you, my God.

My soul is thirsting for God,
the God of my life;
when can I enter and see
the face of God?

My tears have become my bread,
by night, by day,
as I hear it said all the day long:
"Where is your God?"

These things will I remember
as I pour out my soul:
how I would lead the rejoicing crowd
into the house of God,
amid cries of gladness and thanksgiving,
the throng wild with joy

(42: 1–4).

The poet expresses his grief and longing in an image of incomparable beauty. Looking for words to describe his painful need for God, he thinks of the deer, which, in the blazing hot summer, stretches its neck out as far as possible in its search for water in the dried up streams and pools. He identifies with the pain of the deer because he himself is reaching out to God with all his heart, in his own spiritual dryness. God is the "God of my life", or "the Living God", for God has become his most important relationship. His whole life centres around God, so his sense of loss is great. He longs to see the face of God again. This does not imply a face-to-face seeing, which is not given in this life; it means that the poet wishes to present himself before the presence of God in the Temple, far away in Jerusalem (see Deuteronomy 31:11). He feels that it is only there that he can have full communion with God (v. 2).

His anguish increases as the unbelievers taunt and mock him daily, asking: "where is your God?" The pagans of those times mocked the Israelites for worshipping a God

who could not be seen, and who did not allow represen-
tations of Himself to be made. All the pagan religions had
idols which could be carried about, so that it did not matter
where they were supposed to live. The problem for the
Israelite was that he believed, wrongly, that God could
only be found in the Temple in Jerusalem. This crisis will be
answered by the psalm itself, as the Levite discovers that he
is in spiritual communion with God. No one can take this
privilege away from a child of God.

However, the Levite feels very vulnerable before these
pagans, because he has declared his faith. He is not like the
camel, able to survive the desert drought. He is the stricken
deer, worn out by his longing for the living waters of God's
grace, God's Word, and God's life. He does not even
realize that he is among those called "blessed" by Jesus
because they hunger and thirst for what is right, or those
who believe without seeing (see Matthew 5:4, John 20:29).
He does not understand the deceptive ease of the worldly
people around him, who have their fill now, people who
know nothing of this painful longing for God, which is a
deep grace.

Trying to relieve the pain, the poet relives those
wonderful scenes in the Temple during the great festivals,
when he had the privilege of leading the processions into
the House of God. He loved the excitement of the great
ceremonies, and felt the sense of the presence of God when
the people offered their shouts of joy and praise (v. 4).

Why are you cast down, my soul,
why groan within me?
Hope in God; I will praise him still,
my saviour and my God.

My soul is cast down within me
as I think of you,
from the country of Jordan and Mount Hermon,
from the Hill of Mizar.

Deep is calling on deep,
in the roar of waters:
your torrents and all your waves
swept over me.

By day the Lord will send
his loving kindness;
by night I will sing to him,
praise the God of my life
(vv. 5–8).

During the time lost in reverie the Levite found relief from
his distress. Now as he returns to reality he plunges into
depression and an even greater sense of loss. In a touching
dialogue with himself, he soon realizes that all this day
spent dreaming about "the good old days" did not help him
to deal with the problem on hand. Healing lies in facing the
reality of the present moment with the strength that comes
from God. He must learn to do what all the saints had done
before him, namely, to wait on God, and also to wait for
God's perfect timing for things to resolve themselves. He
needs the advice of Isaiah 40:31: "They that hope (wait) in
the Lord will renew their strength, they will soar as with
eagles' wings; They shall run and not grow weary, walk and
not grow faint" (N.A.B.). This means that the Levite must
bear the whole tension of his life in faith and trust before
God, until he experiences God coming to him as saviour in
this situation, as He has done in all others. Only then will he
be able to testify to God's goodness again (v. 5).

What is so attractive about this Levite is the honesty with
which he reveals his inner struggle. While he tries to take
hold of himself with faith and hope, he continually falls
back into his home-sickness for Jerusalem and his need for
God's presence. His struggle is real, and he falls many
times before his final victory. He cannot see any beauty in
this place of exile. Neither the grandeur of Mount Hermon
nor the sight of the origin of the Jordan river, with its

cascading waters tumbling down the mountain, has any effect on him. His thoughts are on the little Mount Zion in Jerusalem. He ruefully refers to Hermon as "Mizar", which means a "little" mountain; obviously its natural grandeur could not compare with the privilege of Mount Zion, which houses the Living God (v. 6; see also Psalm 68:16–17).

This thought plunges him again into trouble as he resonates with the waters of the Jordan plunging into the valley below over the roaring cataracts. He feels that he has lost his foothold and is being carried along with those raging torrents of pain and sorrow; he wonders if this could be the hand of God in punishment (v. 7). Even if it is, he will stretch out his own hand to God yet again! This deeply moving candour and simplicity is the way out for this sufferer. In spite of everything, including his own inability to remain faithful to God in quiet trust and hope, he acts in faith that the loving-kindness of God will reach him again. Therefore he will continue, day and night, to praise God. He is determined, with God's help, to persevere in faith and trust (v. 8).

> I will say to God my rock:
> "Why have you forgotten me?
> Why do I go mourning
> oppressed by the foe?"
>
> With cries that pierce me to the heart,
> my enemies revile me,
> saying to me all the day long:
> "Where is your God?"
>
> Why are you cast down, my soul,
> why groan within me?
> Hope in God; I will praise him still,
> my saviour and my God
>
> (vv. 9–11).

The Levite realizes that there is no solution for him apart from God, yet God appears to be absent. His dilemma is that for him God is a rock to lean on, unshakeable, durable and faithful. He leans on God in faith, while trying to grapple with the unanswered problem as to why God has abandoned him. The mystery deepens (v. 9). To be oppressed by inward doubts and anxiety is trial enough, without the added taunts of unbelievers outside. Their scornful questioning as to where his God is, only serves to deepen his own doubts, and sense of loneliness.

This first half of the psalm ends with the repetition of the refrain, which sounds like the Levite's last desperate effort to cling on to God come what may. It is a reminder of Jacob clinging on to the angel after a night of struggle, when he said: "I will not let you go, unless you bless me" (Genesis 32:26).

15

Psalm 43:
Towards a Solution

Defend me, O God, and plead my cause
against a godless nation.
From deceitful and cunning men
rescue me, O God.

Since you, O God, are my stronghold,
why have you rejected me?
Why do I go mourning
oppressed by the foe?

O send forth your light and your truth;
let these be my guide.
Let them bring me to your holy mountain
to the place where you dwell.

And I will come to the altar of God,
the God of my joy.
My redeemer, I will thank you on the harp,
O God, my God.

Why are you cast down, my soul,
why groan within me?
Hope in God; I will praise him still,
my saviour and my God.

(vv. 1–5).

The struggle in the heart of the Levite has reached a
different stage now, which enables him to pass victoriously
through the darkness, to stand in the quiet assurance of

faith and trust that his prayer is being answered. He holds firmly on to the reality of God's presence – with him now. He prays that God will vindicate him before his foes, will let these godless people see that the Lord is God indeed, and will deliver him out of their hand. He seems unaware that he has transcended his great problem – his belief that God could only be found in the Temple in Jerusalem. God is here with him now, in his trouble.

The limits of his faith are shown, however, when he insists on a physical return to the Temple. He does not yet appreciate the deeper answer he has been given. He requests God to send both light and truth to guide his steps homeward, to God's house. There he will offer joyful sacrifice again and join the choirs in their praise and worship. Now that he can visualize himself back home in the Temple, he calms down. The struggle ceases, and his faith can soar again. His outward circumstances have not changed at all, yet he sees everything differently, for he himself has changed interiorly.

We have much to learn about prayer from this psalm; for the interior struggle with our doubts, with our inability to trust God, with trials which emanate from our contact with the unbelieving world and from the dark caverns of our own soul, are the bread and butter of the spiritual journey. Few are as open and truthful about their interior struggles as this son of Korah, and later St Paul in the New Testament. Both were great men of faith who confronted the reality before them, and were unafraid to speak about their experiences. Because of them, and others like them, lesser souls will gain the courage to face their own particular struggle, and persevere through to victory.

The basis on which the spiritual life is built is longing for God. Without this sense of need there is nothing to build on. Those who experience no need of God are not usually found seeking God in prayer, or longing to participate in community praise and worship. This type usually belong to the group who taunt the others with the scornful question:

"Where is your God?" They say that there is no God, that it is all a myth invented to keep people happy, and to give the neurotic a ray of hope. For them, money, good health, and success in the world supply their needs. They possess no key to understand the grieving of a soul that has truly found God, and fallen in love with Him. To the unbelieving person it is inconceivable that you could be in love with the infinite. They prefer to tell you that you are sick! Sadly, one realizes that the blind cannot lead anyone, let alone another blind person (see Matthew 15:14).

For the soul who is in love with God, life is seen from a very different aspect to that of the unbeliever, or that of the religious person who is not spiritual. One knows the deep interior joy of communion with God, and has the happiness of fellowship with God's friends in His Church. To love, and be loved by, God is the greatest happiness we can know this side of Heaven. Next to that is to know and love the body of Christ on earth, and to be known and recognized as part of this mystery.

For this person the liturgical celebrations of the great feasts of the Church are not empty rituals. They are re-enactments of the great mysteries of our faith, releasing the living waters of grace to the soul, flooding it with joy and peace, whilst nurturing it at the same time, and thus enabling it to grow to full maturity in Christ. To be one with the Lord, and with His body the Church, is the full communion that releases the glory of God to come down in a flood-tide of divine mercy on the whole world.

This soul, knowing and loving God and the brethren, is characterized by a deep longing for God, which is both painful and sweet at the same time. There is no room for self-complacency, for it sees the long road ahead to full union with God. It sees its own sinfulness, which causes it deep anguish, yet it is ravished by the beauty and glory of God, and it longs more and more to see the face of God. This can only come about when the veil of the flesh is removed by death, so the person finds himself longing to be gone and to be with Christ, yet he must stay to accomplish God's will on earth. This tension is a deep, but peaceful suffering (see 2 Corinthians 5:1–4).

The love affair with God is not all joy. It has its times of harrowing darkness, desolation and apparent abandonment by God. This is necessary for growth. We can go for months, or even years with nothing but tears for our lot, day and night. We might even feel that there is no deliverance for us from the dark tunnel of dryness and desolation in prayer. During this time both faith and motivation are purified, until we learn to seek God for Himself alone, not for any selfish reasons. In fact, one who did not have a real love for God would not persevere through this trial. Many go off, like the rich young man in the gospel, thinking that God is unfair to ask such a thing of weak human beings. Some of them join the scoffers, saying that there is no God. For the soul who truly loves, this trial is deepened by the fact that its inward suffering is reinforced by all the unbelief, doubts and agnosticism of friends and neighbours.

Nevertheless, it is fatal to look back to "the good old days" when we enjoyed God's presence, had wonderful retreats, superb conferences, where "things were really happening", where we got a lot out of our prayer and spiritual reading. This merely causes deeper sadness and enhances the sense of loss, which is bad enough already. Victory lies in denying oneself the luxury of daydreaming, and deciding to stay in the reality of the present moment, where the grace of God is ever present to help us. Here St Paul's advice, ". . . to bring every thought into captivity, to make it obedient to Christ" (N.A.B.), is very helpful if we do not want to lose our peace.

One of the great secrets of success in the spiritual journey is to discover the grace of the present moment. God revealed Himself to Moses as "the great I am", the God of the eternal now. When we revert to the past, or fantasize regarding the future, we miss the opportunities that lie under our feet for making the most of the reality of our present circumstances. We may even miss some important grace God had planned for us, and so, needlessly, lengthen our spiritual journey. Jesus taught this to Martha in John 11, when she did just this regarding her dead brother, Lazarus. "If only you had been here . . . Yes, I know he will rise on the last day . . ." She almost missed seeing the glory of God work through her present bereavement.

God is with us now, even in our dark tunnels, and He is resurrection and life for us. As we let His light penetrate into our deepest depths, we gradually emerge fully resurrected, alive, and healed in our innermost being. And our life remains "hidden with Christ in God", safe now from the taunts and the gaze of the unbelievers (see Colossians 1:1–3).

Resistance to grace at this point merely deepens the pain while lengthening the journey. Thus dragged all the way to Calvary, we leave our heel-marks on the track, so that all other pilgrims will know that we have passed this way! Nothing is achieved by it. To wait on God in faith, trust and surrender to the operations of His grace in us, no matter how mysterious, is the sure and quick way to victory. To wait in joyful hope on God's action and on God's perfect timing in our lives is a hard lesson to master, because the "God knows best" attitude comes with difficulty to the adult, who instinctively prefers self-reliance to the seemingly ridiculous stance of surrender to God's will. But when the lesson is mastered, we begin to experience God as our unshakeable rock, the One who will never fail us or forsake us. We walk forward then in tranquil, joyful faith. The outward circumstances in our life may not have changed yet everything is different, and we are no longer wounded by the taunts of others.

We now understand more fully the words of Psalm 46:10: "Be still and know that I am God." We can stand aside now and watch God vindicate us in situations that we thought impossible. He protects us from spiritual and earthly enemies, because we allow Him to, while at the same time, as our teacher and guide, He leads us into all truth. He will not give up the training programme until He brings us to the top of the mountain.

16

Psalm 50:
True Worship

The author of this psalm, Asaph, writes poetry that is direct, vigorous, confident, powerful and regal. Unlike Korah, who was demoted from the Temple, Asaph and his house were put in charge of the Temple liturgy, a position which he and his descendants held right into the post-exilic era (see 1 Chronicles 25:1–2, Ezra 3:10). The psalm itself has the character of a liturgy, where the main section consists of a divine utterance of judgement delivered in the style of a prophetic rebuke. God Himself appears among them to sit in judgement. But if all eyes are upon Him, His eyes are upon Israel.

The whole psalm is addressed to the covenant people; first to the unthinking religious, then to the hardened and the hypocritical, to bring them to their senses. This is reality therapy, where God makes his people see things as they really are. It is the message which the prophets, and finally Jesus, tried to get through to Israel, and the Church, lest they forget, involved in all their lovely liturgies, that they were dealing with the living God.

The features of the psalm recalling the covenant on Sinai (vv. 1–5), allusions to the ten commandments (vv. 7,18–20), and to allegiance to the covenant (v. 16), combine to set this psalm in the festival of the covenant. The essence of the Covenant renewal was not sacrifice, but the surrender of the heart to God in obedience to His Commandments, and to the stipulations of the Covenant.

> The God of gods, the Lord,
> has spoken and summoned the earth,
> from the rising of the sun to its setting.
> Out of Sion's perfect beauty he shines.

(Our God comes, he keeps silence no longer.)

Before him fire devours,
around him tempest rages.
He calls on the heavens and the earth
to witness his judgement of his people.

"Summon before me my people
who made covenant with me by sacrifice."
The heavens proclaim his justice,
for he, God, is the judge

(vv. 1–6).

The psalm opens with a great theophany in the Temple. Somehow God manifests His powerful presence during the liturgical ceremonies, a presence reminiscent of that given to Moses on Sinai (see Exodus 3:19), or to Elijah (1 Kings 19:9–18), or Isaiah (Isaiah 6:1–6), or even Ezekiel (Ezekiel chapter 1). Asaph here describes how God acts, rather than how He appears to them, because God has come to sit in judgement over His covenant people. As God of the universe He summons all peoples to witness this trial. He is in special relationship with Israel because of the covenant, yet, to their amazement, the pagan nations are called in as the jury! They had never grasped that God had plans for the rest of mankind too. The Israelites have failed to allow themselves to be spiritually affected, touched or transformed by God's presence among them. The pagan world will now bear witness against them for their privileged status, and for their failure to respond to it (v. 1).

God is now in their midst, the perfection of beauty, light and glory, and Mount Sion reflects this because the Temple was situated there. Asaph is obviously speaking about a time when the Temple worship was in full bloom (v. 2). The prophet among them speaks out now that God should hold His silence no longer, for the people need the rebuke that is coming to them. Recalling Sinai he reminds the people that

God is majestic and awesome, that He comes as a devouring fire or tempest, so that the people should tremble before Him in humility and a proper fear (see Exodus 19:16–25, 1 Kings 19:11ff). Awesome reverence is the correct attitude in anyone who really knows who God is.

Moses warned the people what would happen in the event of their breaking the covenant; we find his prophecy fulfilled here, as God calls heaven and earth to witness the trial of His people (see Deuteronomy 30:19). As St Peter told the infant Church later, judgement must "begin with the Household of God" (see 1 Peter 4:17). Both Israel and the Church must face the responsibility that goes with their privileged status before God, for "to whom much is given much is expected" (see Luke 12:48). Israel may think she is fine in her own eyes, but in this trial her justification before the ultimate authority is at stake. The reason for the trial was that the people, as a nation, had solemnly bound themselves to God by sacrifice to keep the covenant made with their consent on Mount Sinai (see Exodus 24:4–8). This had placed them in a unique relationship with God, different from all other peoples, but their history shows that they preferred the privileges to the responsibilities incumbent on them. Now the moment of truth has come . . . (vv. 4–6).

> "Listen, my people, I will speak;
> Israel, I will testify against you,
> for I am God your God.
> I accuse you, lay the charge before you.
>
> I find no fault with your sacrifices,
> your offerings are always before me.
> I do not ask more bullocks from your farms,
> nor goats from among your herds.
>
> For I own all the beasts of the forest,
> beasts in their thousands on my hills.
> I know all the birds in the sky,
> all that moves in the field belong to me.

Were I hungry, I would not tell you,
for I own the world and all it holds.
Do you think I eat the flesh of bulls,
or drink the blood of goats?

Pay your sacrifice of thanksgiving to God
and render him your votive offerings.
Call on me in the day of distress.
I will free you and you shall honour me"

(vv. 7–15).

God here reveals to His people that their cardinal sin is that they resort to ritual while refusing Him the relationship which alone can give inner reality to the offering. It is mindless religion; they seek to keep God "happy" with sacrifices and ritual while refusing to repent and let God save them. This type of religion tends to end up in empty ritual and legalistic formalism, the sin of the Pharisee at a later date, perhaps the sin of many Christians today? (see 2 Timothy 3:5). But God wants to be taken seriously, and He wants us to realize who He is! (v. 7).

It is not the sacrifices themselves, nor their zeal in offering them, that God finds fault with. Indeed, so many sacrifices were offered that God said they were continually before Him! The problem lies in the fact that the people think that God needs their sacrifices, and is, therefore, dependent on them for their gifts and prayers. They reveal the depth of their insecurity here; they made themselves independent of God, they tried to "control" God by their sacrifices, rituals and prayers so that He would obey the will of His creatures instead of them obeying Him. Thus they have turned religion upside down!

Our true position before God is very different. God is independent of His creatures, as He reveals here, and He cannot and will not be manipulated by them. Sacrifices and rituals represent our need, not God's. It is prideful arrogance that seeks to put man on an equal footing with God. It is preposterous even to think that God needed to eat, and somehow fed on the animal sacrifices; this type of thinking showed that man had lost sight of the majesty, glory and other-worldliness of God. Hence the theophany was needed to re-educate the people to the fact that God is *pure spirit*, and needs nothing from His creatures (vv. 8–13).

The response required of us by God is not pomp and ceremony but love, and surrender to His will and to His redeeming work in us. He looks for the sacrifice of praise coming from the depths of the heart (see Hebrews 13:15). This type of worship acknowledges God as the most high and gives Him due honour, while enabling us to have a stance of humility before Him. The people must recognize their dependence on God, and call on Him for deliverance in their troubles. The prayer of the heart, not ritual, gets through to God, because God wants to be worshipped in spirit and in truth (see John 4:21–24).

(But God says to the wicked:)

"But how can you recite my commandments
and take my covenant on your lips,
you who despise my law
and throw my words to the winds,

you who see a thief and go with him;
who throw in your lot with adulterers,
who unbridle your mouth for evil
and whose tongue is plotting crime,

you who sit and malign your brother
and slander your own mother's son.
You do this, and should I keep silence?
Do you think that I am like you?

Mark this, you who never think of God,
lest I seize you and you cannot escape;
a sacrifice of thanksgiving honours me
and I will show God's salvation to the upright"
(vv. 16–23).

These verses are addressed, not to the pagan nations who
are present to witness this trial of God's people, but to the
nominally orthodox, those members of the covenant community who neglect their duty to God, and therefore
neglect to obey His commandments. If the last group
addressed in verses 7–15 needed a reminder that God was
spiritual, this group in verses 16–21 need to be told that
God is moral, and demands a true inward response to the
covenant. The first group were corrected in their response
to the first half of the Decalogue, regarding their relationship with God. This group need enlightenment on the
second half of the Decalogue, which deals with our relationship with our neighbour. This has always been part of
our service to God, for the whole law is summed up in
loving God and our neighbour (see Deuteronomy 6:5,
Leviticus 19:18, Matthew 22:34–40).

This second group fall into the category of those who are
prepared to study the Law, even teach it to others, but who,
because they hate discipline, never put it into practice.
There was nothing wrong with their theology – just with
their behaviour. They were denounced by the prophets,
and later by Jesus, as hypocrites (see Isaiah 29:13,
Jeremiah 8:8, Matthew 5:20). For them God's Law was a
subject for discussion and debate rather than obedience.
Unfortunately for them God's judgement deals with behaviour and not theology! (see Matthew 25). Like the first
group, these people have a wrong concept of God.
Thinking that God acts like a human being, they misinter-
pret His silence, patience and lack of retribution. They
equate their own will with God's will, because they do not
see God as He really is, nor do they consider His right to

their absolute obedience. They too have trivialized God, and made Him into their own image. This is their sin; again this is upside-down religion. Now they are confronted by God in this theophany as He really is, and their eyes are opened to their true obligations before Him. If they will not change, they must face the wrath of God for breaking their vows to Him. He will show them who is master and lord. Should they repent, they will find Him a true saviour. The choice is theirs.

Two fundamental problems of the spiritual life are touched upon in this psalm. The first is that we try to make God into our own image, and think that by prayer, fasting, almsgiving and other good works, we can somehow manipulate and control God. The second is that we think that the externals of religion, namely liturgy and ritual, make us very religious people, and somehow keep God happy. In this second misconception we find that we have a serious, but very common, problem. By our observance of the externals of religion we can deceive ourselves into thinking that we are true servants of God. In fact, liturgy is necessary to express our worship to God, but if it is devoid of the spiritual content, the dynamism that energizes it, then it becomes empty formalism. At best liturgy should express the attitude of the surrender of the heart to God, as well as our humility before Him, and our praise. Unfortunately many people think that there is some "magic" about going through the ritual itself; they are in danger of thinking that they are serving God, when they may be closed to the challenge of His Word, and be unrepentant in several areas of their lives. If they persist in this attitude they may think that they are doing God a service by going to church, in which case they would have God dependent on man instead of the other way around. Meanwhile the invitation of God remains the same: "My son, give me your heart, and let your eyes keep to my ways" (Proverbs 23:26; N.A.B.).

For many nominal Christians, it is like being in a club or a political party; they follow the party line on doctrine and theology, but live private lives that contradict the very doctrines they hold! Religion devoid of morality is monstrous, mere fuel for scoffers, lacking any reality or living testimony to the presence and the glory of God. Jesus had hard words for the Pharisees on this point: they occupied the chair of Moses, but did not practise what they preached. Jesus uncovered their sins in public – just as in this psalm – so that the people became aware of their refusal to surrender to God or obey His Law (see Matthew 23:1–36). They kept to the rituals but neglected the weightier matters of the Law concerning justice, mercy, good faith and forgiveness.

Further along the spiritual path we find others who have gone through a conversion experience, are sincerely seeking God and praying, yet they too can think that their prayer, fasting, almsgiving and other good works can manipulate God into doing what they ask. For example, they pray sincerely for a sick person's healing, but their attitude is that God "ought to" or "must" heal the person *because* they have prayed and fasted. The thinking behind it is the same, that God somehow needs our prayer and fasting to do this work of mercy. It is an important enlightenment when we discover who God is; then we realize that He can in no way be manipulated and controlled by any amount of prayer and fasting. If our prayer and fasting is sincere, God will enlighten us to the fact that His perfect will for this person is the greatest thing we can pray for, because it includes the salvation of the whole person. The greatest grace we can ask for is the fullness of redemption to be manifested in the person, and if this includes the healing of the body, then amen. One must question whether the "demand" for healing in particular cases is not just an ego trip, to show to others the power of *my* prayers or "my ministry", instead of being concerned with the ultimate good of the person, and with the glory of God.

This psalm shows us that God wants a people who will know Him, will relate to Him personally; a people who will worship Him in spirit and in truth, a people who will keep His commandments, and whatever vows they have contracted in His presence. In return He will be a God of mercy and compassion.

17

Psalm 51:
The Joy of True Repentance

Among the penitential psalms this one is the most important because it captures the essence of true repentance. It
grasps the real depths of sin and shows the way unerringly
to restored communion with God. With Romans 7 in the
New Testament it has deep insight into the struggles of the
human heart during a great spiritual battle. David wrote
this psalm after Nathan, the prophet, had called him to
account for his adultery with Bathsheba, and the murder of
her husband (see 2 Samuel 11:12). The last two verses are a
later addition to the psalm, when it was re-interpreted after
the Exile at the time of the rebuilding of the Temple,
somewhere between 539 and 445 BC.

> Have mercy on me, God, in your kindness.
> In your compassion blot out my offence.
> O wash me more and more from my guilt
> and cleanse me from my sin
>
> (vv. 1–2).

Full of distress David turns imploringly to God and asks for
mercy, that very special quality of loving-kindness in the
heart of God which opens the way for sinners to be reconciled
with Him. Mercy is that quality of "bending over backwards"
by which God reaches out with forgiveness and salvation to
the sinner. To this special love of God David appeals successfully. Were he not so conscious of this divine mercy he might
have broken under the sheer weight of his guilt. He has such a
tremendous sense of sinfulness that it does not occur to him to
appeal to past integrity, as happens so often in the psalms.

This time he knows that there is no hope for him outside divine mercy. Only God can blot out his sin, and cleanse his soul from its defilement. He knows that forgiveness is not enough. He must be thoroughly cleansed, so that there is no recurrence of the problem. He begs God, therefore, to see him through his rehabilitation.

> My offences truly I know them;
> my sin is always before me.
> Against you, you alone, have I sinned;
> what is evil in your sight I have done.
>
> That you may be justified when you give sentence
> and be without reproach when you judge,
> O see, in guilt I was born,
> a sinner was I conceived.
>
> Indeed you love truth in the heart;
> then in the secret of my heart teach me wisdom
>
> (vv. 3–6).

The first step on the road to conversion is self-knowledge, and David is well and truly there. His is not the momentary sorrow of one who will go away forgetting what has happened. Instead, it is the deep shock that true self-knowledge brings, the shock of the responsibility one bears before God and one's neighbour. Confronted in prayer with the reality of God's presence he confesses his sin, acknowledging his rebellion before God. Yet it is obvious that he does not expect the wrath of God to come upon him, for he speaks with such simplicity, candour and truthfulness that he reveals a deep love for God in spite of his sin. He knows, too, that the depth of healing will depend on the extent to which he opens the real wound to God.

Seeing his sins, even those against his neighbour, in the wider setting, David realizes that all sin is basically rebellion against God. Obedience to God's will in this case would have ensured the safety and freedom of Uriah and his wife. As it is, both of them have lost everything. Suddenly David becomes aware of being caught in a twofold mystery: the majesty of God, and His right to judge David for his actions on the one hand; and on the other, he sees that God has used the present pain to arouse the sinner to come to Him in his helplessness, so that mercy and forgiveness, rather than judgement, can be given. Thus it is in the recognition of his sinfulness that David comes to understand God better, both in the seriousness of His dealings with us, and in the greatness of His loving mercy. This same principle still holds good for today (see Romans 11:30–32).

On reviewing his life David realizes that "sinner" is our true title, because from our birth we entered a world of sinful and sinning humanity, a world full of good and evil. The tendency to self-will and rebellion shows early in life, and we need no schooling in this! All our other sins find their roots here, and if they are not checked, we shall become addicted to self-glorification and self-advancement, both of which the unbelieving world considers to be normal behaviour. This insight given to David by God, in prayer, is the beginning of wisdom. It is given to all who sincerely seek God. This truth about the reality of the human condition is felt, at first, to be humiliating, but ultimately it leads to our liberation, for when we throw ourselves on God's mercy it releases His power and grace into our souls, to purify us from all sin, not just this specific sin. Like a good gardener God prefers to pull up the weeds by the roots.

O purify me, then I shall be clean;
O wash me, I shall be whiter than snow.

Make me hear rejoicing and gladness,
that the bones you have crushed may thrill.
From my sins turn away your face
and blot out all my guilt

(vv. 7–9).

Comforted by God's response in receiving him, and by the revelation just granted, David cries out again to be purified from his sin, until his soul has fully recovered from the fall. Thinking of the rites for the purification of lepers, and sinners, where they were sprinkled with the blood of the sacrificial animal using a hyssop stick, David desires the utter joy of the leper who has just been declared clean (see Leviticus 14:4–6, Luke 17:16, Mark 1:45). Joy and gladness well up in the heart of the cleansed sinner too, in the realization of the undeserved forgiveness received, and also because the burden of guilt and shame that oppressed them has been lifted.

> A pure heart create for me, O God,
> put a steadfast spirit within me.
> Do not cast me away from your presence,
> nor deprive me of your holy spirit.
>
> Give me again the joy of your help;
> with a spirit of fervour sustain me,
> that I may teach transgressors your ways
> and sinners may return to you
>
> (vv. 10–13).

At this point David sees that forgiveness and mercy are not enough. He needs to be given strength and wisdom to face the future with a different attitude to life. He knows that he cannot sustain a life of virtue without God's help, for he is aware of the tendency to slip back into the old habits. He needs the gift of fortitude and a steadfast spirit to enable him to persevere in doing good. Only God can transform the human heart, so David requests this now (see Jeremiah 31:31–33, Ezekiel 36:25ff).

Remembering the sad events that ended the life of King Saul, his predecessor, David now pleads with God not to remove the Holy Spirit from him (see 1 Samuel 16:14). To be cast out of God's presence and deprived of His guidance and protection would be the ultimate punishment, which David realizes will happen if he perseveres in rebellion against God. To enjoy God's presence is the great boast of God's friends, since the time of Abraham to the present day. We carry the wonder of His promise, "I will be with you", everywhere we go. This gives us access to God in prayer at any time and in any place. To be deprived of this privilege would cause unthinkable anguish in anyone who had ever known God (see Exodus 3:12, Matthew 28:20, etc).

Only God can raise us from servile obedience based on fear to a joyful loving commitment to His will. This is what is requested now so that David can become a joyful messenger of good news to others (see Acts 4:20). It is a true conversion that turns so completely from sin to concentrate on helping to prevent others from going down the same slippery slope that caused his own downfall. David will confirm his conversion by teaching others the way of righteousness he has just learned.

> O rescue me, God, my helper,
> and my tongue shall ring out your goodness.
> O Lord, open my lips
> and my mouth shall declare your praise.
>
> For in sacrifice you take no delight,
> burnt offering from me you would refuse,
> my sacrifice, a contrite spirit.
> A humbled, contrite heart you will not spurn
> (vv. 14–17).

At this point David asks to be delivered from danger – perhaps the danger of death. He realizes that everything comes from the hand of God as pure gift, both his life and his ability to praise God again, but it is God who must open his lips so that praise can come forth, for he now knows his utter dependence on God for all his good. It was the custom

113

to offer thanksgiving sacrifices to God at that time (see Leviticus 7:12, 22:29, Psalm 107:22, etc), and also to make vows, but David breaks out from this mould and boldly states that the "circumcision of the heart" is more pleasing to God than all the sacrifices he could offer (see Jeremiah 4:4, Romans 2:29). He knows that our relationship with God is wholly spiritual and that conversion of heart and surrender to God are the essential elements in it. The prophets concur with this teaching; they tried to uncover for the people their underlying motivation in worship and called for the conversion of the heart as the essential element of religion (see Amos 5:21–26, Hosea 6:6, etc). True conversion is a lifelong commitment of surrender to God, where the greatest personal sacrifice we can render to God is the sacrifice of our self-will; indeed it is the only one truly pleasing to Him. Here David has picked up the essential element, offering sacrifice, and raised it to its highest spiritual peak.

> In your goodness, show favour to Sion:
> rebuild the walls of Jerusalem.
> Then you will be pleased with lawful sacrifice,
> (burnt offerings wholly consumed),
> then you will be offered young bulls on your altar
> (vv. 18–19).

It is generally agreed that these last verses were an addition to the psalm in the post-exilic era when the Temple was being rebuilt and the sacrificial cult restored. Amazingly it misinterprets the psalm. The author of the appendix wants the teaching of the psalm to be interpreted in the light of the absence of the sacrificial cult during the Exile, and expresses the hope that now, in its restoration, God will receive "right" and "proper" sacrifices. He does not realize that there is only one more sacrifice that God wants to receive, namely that of the Messiah, given for the redemption of the world.

114

This psalm reveals a fundamental breakthrough in the spiritual life, one that releases us from being "religious" to being truly spiritual. It comes through radically facing one's own sinfulness, through the gate of self-knowledge. In a general way we all acknowledge ourselves to be sinners. We may be deeply religious and yet there can be attitudes in us that prevent us from making progress, even though we may belong to a prayer group and claim to be walking in the Spirit.

God, in His mercy, has to allow us to come up against the wall of self-will, stubbornness, rebellion, and our refusal to listen to advice, before we will face our sinfulness in a radical way. He has to permit circumstances that show up our resistance to grace, our self-glorification in our so-called good deeds, and our complacency in being "good" and "religious", unlike the rest of men. Not until we are confronted by this mass of evidence will we face the conversion that is called for. If the sight of our sinfulness merely depresses us we show that we are still not ready for the moment of grace. Only when the pain and the shame drive us into the loving arms of Jesus are we ready to discover the One who is the friend of outcasts and sinners (see Luke 5:29–32). He will receive us, but we must come before Him in truth, in humility and self-distrust. In persevering prayer God will show us the roots of sin, and reveal to us life-long habits of sin – attitudes that we have adopted and accepted as part of our personality – that are not until now seen as sinful at all. To face our radical innate sinfulness is a great grace. Like David, we then see that we need far more than forgiveness if we are to be set free, and we, too, will ask for the deep cleansing of our souls and the purification of the heart which is so essential to the true service of God. We may also need re-education in our habits which are not changed easily. As we struggle to come free, we shall go through a stage of always seeing our sin before us as David did. Only then can we appreciate the rebellion against God that is involved in the service of

115

the self. As we grow, God will give us insight into our real motivation in our relationships and other situations in life, thus enabling us to savour the deep sinfulness inherent in human nature. The knowledge can be so crushing at times that our health can suffer, and God alone can restore our joy by the gift of His forgiveness, healing and peace.

After many humiliating failures to overcome the all pervasive ego, we realize that God will have to accomplish in us what we cannot do for ourselves. He will have to give us the "new heart and the new spirit" that He promised (see Ezekiel 36:25–26). He alone can give us the inner fortitude to face the struggle and see it through, and He alone can keep us walking a life of virtue. Therefore we ask Him to bring this to pass in us so that it will be all of grace, and all the glory will go to Him.

Realizing that our transgressions are many we develop a deep sense of sinfulness, and our prayer is now laced with humility and reverence (see Isaiah 59:12–13, Jeremiah 14:7–20). We know that our rebellion grieves the Holy Spirit who indwells us, so we beg God to keep us close to Him and let us experience the joy of His continuing work in us (see Isaiah 63:10–11, Ephesians 4:30). At last it dawns upon us that the relationship between God and the individual person is that between a Saviour and a sinner always. This brings great relief, and we can get on with living off God's divine mercy and loving-kindness, and forgetting not only our own "holiness" but ourselves altogether. With this, peace comes at last.

Now we realize how utterly dependent on God we really are. He alone can bring us to true enlightenment that leads to conversion, and the circumcision of the heart. He alone can bring us to true joy and peace, and put the praise of God upon our lips and in our hearts. We surrender to Him utterly, knowing that the humbled contrite heart is indeed pleasing to Him, and that the sacrifice of the surrender of the self is the only gift He asks of us. When it is given, He can use us to teach others the way of peace, and help to rebuild His Church.

18

Psalm 62:
The Eye of the Storm

David dedicated this psalm to Jeduthun, who was one of the chief musicians appointed by him to lead the public worship (see 1 Chronicles 16:41, 25:1–3). David has worked his way through a deep crisis involving faithless friends, who have now become his persecutors; he has found the eye of the storm in his spiritual life, and shows us how to find it also. His answer came through wrestling with himself and God in prayer, so this psalm has much to teach us about the true spirit of prayer.

It resembles Psalms 42–43 insofar as it shows us David struggling to answer pressing problems through his relationship with God. The difference lies in the fact that here trust in God is the dominant motif, so the difficulties are more easily overcome. He not only attains peace of mind, but also the right level of sound moral judgement on which he can base the rest of his life; out of his own experience he will be able to teach others. His quiet self-mastery comes from his unshakeable trust in God.

In God alone is my soul at rest;
my help comes from him.
He alone is my rock, my stronghold,
my fortress: I stand firm.

How long will you all attack one man
to break him down,
as though he were a tottering wall,
or a tumbling fence?

Their plan is only to destroy:
they take pleasure in lies.
With their mouth they utter blessing
but in their heart they curse.

In God alone be at rest, my soul;
for my hope comes from him.
He alone is my rock, my stronghold,
my fortress: I stand firm.

In God is my safety and glory,
the rock of my strength.
Take refuge in God all you people.
Trust him at all times.
Pour out your hearts before him
for God is our refuge.

Common folk are only a breath,
great men an illusion.
Placed in the scales, they rise;
they weigh less than a breath.

Do not put your trust in oppression
nor vain hopes on plunder.
Do not set your heart on riches
even when they increase.

For God has said only one thing:
only two do I know:
that to God alone belongs power
and to you, Lord, love;
and that you repay each man
according to his deeds

(vv. 1–12).

Like Psalm 23, this lovely prayer carries its entire message
in the first verse. David has been wrestling with God in

prayer because he has been forsaken, and is now persecuted by his former friends. He had sought human help to no avail, and he has no strength in himself, for he feels like a tottering wall. He has now turned to God, the ultimate source of help and strength. There he has found what everyone seeks – true peace of soul. Here it is called "rest", in true biblical terms. The external circumstances of his life have not altered, for the persecution still continues, but he has found a safe haven in God. This inner stillness and peace is the source of his strength to cope with his troubles. It was not until he fixed his attention on God alone that the inner turmoil came to rest. The presence of God is his strength now. He stands on the everlasting rock that is God; he remains unmoved by the trouble because he has found a firm footing in God. His former anxiety is resolved and replaced by an unswerving confidence in God (vv. 1–2).

At this point David can afford to let us see the extent of his pain and bitter disappointment over the former friends who are trying to bring him down. He is fully conscious of the calamitous situation that he is in, which is shown by the graphic description of himself as a tottering wall or a tumbling fence, either of which could be destroyed without effort. His own weakness does not disturb him, since he is leaning on God's strength. He views his adversaries with quiet detachment, seeing through their scheming and hypocritical behaviour, for they still pretend to be his friends. From his new standpoint in God he can see clearly what is happening around him, but he is not afraid (vv. 3–4).

His thoughts return to God again. He refuses to allow the presence of his enemies to disturb his peace of soul. He returns quietly to the source of his strength, God, and draws from Him the grace he needs to master his inner turmoil (vv. 5–6).

Having found the answer to his own difficulties, David desires to share his joy and peace with others. Turning to all believers he implores them to throw themselves on God's mercy in prayer, and trust Him to bring the solution to their personal problems. To pour out your heart to God in prayer is to open yourself up completely, allowing God to work in you and in your life, just as David did so effectively (vv. 7–8).

Deep in meditation now, David discovers that our values and standards change radically when seen from God's point of view. We may have an elevated opinion of ourselves in the world, but the presence of God enables us truly to evaluate our worth. We weigh less than a breath! What marvellous vision! The glory of man and his achievements shrinks into its natural nothingness before the majesty, greatness, immensity and glory of God, the creator. Great men are seen in their true worth, and we learn not to trust human nature, which can be so contradictory. The profundity of David's insight here is due to the fact that, in deep prayer, helped by the Holy Spirit, he can get to the root of things, of human nature and of himself. We see reality as it really is in God's sight, where all camouflage and deception are removed. To have the courage to stand naked before God's truth is a great grace. As a result we put our hope in God rather than in man, and in the power of God rather than in money. The corrupting influence of both power and money are seen for what they are, and David warns us not to fall into this worldly mire (vv. 9–10).

In the final verses David offers some guidance for our lives. The person of faith knows in his heart that power and strength belong to God, while weakness and sinfulness are native to us. The good news is that God's power works best through our human weakness when we surrender to the operations of His grace in us. The power of God working through the surrendered soul is very great, not only for the salvation of that individual, but also for the redemption of the world (see 1 Corinthians 1:26–31, 2 Corinthians 12:9–10).

There are some profound insights into prayer in this

psalm, but it is fairly advanced prayer that is under discussion. The soul is undergoing a deep trial, through which the Lord is purifying it. The means of purification come from everyday life, where God uses the ordinary circumstances of our day and the people we live with as His instruments, His "ways and means" committee! To meet with deceitfulness and hypocrisy in those we love or work with is difficult to handle. It may seem at times that everyone is getting at us at once. The secret is to fly to God in prayer, not superficial prayer where we just say words to God, but the profound prayer of the aching heart. We go into "that inner room" Jesus spoke about, where the heart is engaged deeply with God, where we listen to Him, where we can touch the heart of God and draw to ourselves His peace (see Matthew 6:6). Thus strengthened we emerge with our inner turmoil stilled and able to cope with the difficult situation on hand. This prayer is not just talking to God, even though initially it may begin with words. It means relating to God as saviour in the here and now. It is a very practical, demanding, deep faith and trust in God. When we can truthfully say, "in God alone I find rest for my soul", we are progressing, for then we have learned to lean on God for grace and strength in the nitty gritty of everyday life. The spiritual life is fought out in our homes and work places, not in church, as many suppose. When we live out our daily lives resting on the unshakeable rock that is Christ we find we can triumph over all our difficulties.

This heart prayer opens our inner eyes, the eyes of the heart, to true discernment. Indeed one of the signs of growth in prayer is growth in discernment. This is the God-given ability to see things and situations as they really are without the camouflage that normally covers them. It is the ability to see things from God's viewpoint, it enables us to penetrate to the heart of the matter to see the truth, but it does not make one cynical, for God imparts both wisdom and understanding with it.

Instead of becoming cynical we grow in compassion for

others, and in a desire to help them reach their centre in God; we teach them how to pray, so that they, too, can find trust, peace and refuge in God alone. We try to share with them the true values we have learned from God in prayer and by which we discern man's true worth, and see the dreadful emptiness of the worldly way of power, money and the consequent oppression of others. Our glory lies in true surrender to God in faith and love, whereby we enable the power of God to work in us, and through us to spread the kingdom of God on earth. This means, in effect, that we are spreading true joy, peace, fulfilment and happiness and a sense of purpose into many lives. What Good News!

19

Psalm 63:
Longing for God

The secondary title of this psalm "when he was in the wilderness of Judah" seems to refer to the time that David was on the run from King Saul, although some claim that it refers to the revolt of Absolom (see 1 Samuel chaps. 22–24). Those who prefer the latter do so because David refers to himself as "King" in the last verses, and he was not yet crowned king while under King Saul. However, we do know that the psalms were adapted for use in the Temple worship at a later date, so the reference to the king could well be to a later king of Judah, who may have felt alienated and distanced from God by personal or national trials, and the psalm was adapted to suit his needs.

O God, you are my God, for you I long;
for you my soul is thirsting.
My body pines for you
like a dry, weary land without water.
So I gaze on you in the sanctuary
to see your strength and your glory.

For your love is better than life,
my lips will speak your praise.
So I will bless you all my life,
in your name I will lift up my hands.
My soul shall be filled as with a banquet,
my mouth shall praise you with joy.

On my bed I remember you.
On you I muse through the night
for you have been my help;
in the shadow of your wings I rejoice.
My soul clings to you;
your right hand holds me fast.

Those who seek to destroy my life
shall go down to the depths of the earth.
They shall be put into the power of the sword
and left as the prey of the jackals.
But the king shall rejoice in God;
(all that swear by him shall be blessed)
for the mouth of liars shall be silenced

(vv. 1–11).

There is a deep mystic tone in the entire psalm, which shows David in deep crisis yet in great peace before God. Only the mystics know how to marry suffering and joy, tribulation and peace, because their centre is in God. From Him they draw joy, peace and the ability to cope with suffering. If we would but face it as David did, we would see that the deepest pain in the human heart is longing for God, for the infinite, for the ultimate source of life and love. This deep-down ache is felt by everyone, whether they know it or not, and our lives are directed for good or ill depending on how we respond to it (see John 4:13–14). Unfortunately many people do not identify it, so they drown that thirst for the infinite with a life of pleasure or in the pursuit of power, or even in a life that degenerates into violence, none of which satisfies this hunger. It only serves to deepen it while destroying the individual and causing untold harm to others. If this need, "thirst", "hunger" in the depths of our being is faced squarely and directed towards God and our ultimate happiness, then we can reach our full potential.

The God whom we perceive at first to be "out there", at a great distance from us, will soon become "my God", One with whom I am personally relating in deep covenant commitment. Initially the "you are my God" is perceived only vaguely, but as prayer deepens the sense of belonging to God deepens also. This brings a sense of security with it, and confidence in the knowledge of being personally loved by God. At this point the need, felt initially, is now recognized as a personal longing for God as our greatest love, and this love increases the thirst, which in turn drives us deeper into seeking God.

Indeed, it is a great grace to be able to say truthfully that it is for God Himself, and Him only, that we long. This shows that the life is now firmly directed towards its true and ultimate goal. The compass is set for the completion of the journey, just as St Luke shows us Jesus setting His face like flint to go to Jerusalem, and to all that God had destined for Him there (see Luke 9:51) (v. 1).

The wilderness of Judah, in the summertime, is a land that is parched, weary and waterless. This is the graphic description that David uses to describe his need for God. It is the same as saying: "I am an emptiness needing to be filled with the living God. I am dried out and will die unless the living water of God's grace and life comes to give me life. Without God I am nothing, and never can be anything, for 'He is my all'." This inner pain of need overflows into the senses, so that the body, too, echoes this painful thirst for God, which in a strange way is also sweet. The only way to satisfy this lover is somehow to see the face of God, so David longs for the privilege of God's presence in the sanctuary. There he can enter into communion with God before the Holy of Holies which housed the Ark of the Covenant, over which the glory of God manifested itself. It is in this sense that he can see the face of God. He knew that the full vision of God is only given when the veil of the flesh is removed in death (see Exodus 33:20).

In deep communion with God, David will receive grace and strength to handle his difficult situation (v. 2). The mystic knows well that the thirst for God can only be satisfied by deep communion with God in prayer, from which he can draw life, wisdom, grace and discernment to deal with his life. He knows, too, that time is not wasted in prayer, as many suppose it to be. It is a drink from the river of life in the heart of the Lord, a drink that invigorates and heals as well as teaches and gives direction to life.

Considering that, in the wilderness of Judah, David was a fugitive, deprived of both justice and personal freedom; that he was continually hunted there by King Saul who wanted to kill him, simply out of jealousy; that instead of a king's bed in a palace, which was his right, he lay in caves with a stone for his pillow; that he was bereft of all family comforts and rights – considering all this, the next six verses are quite extraordinary. We who read these lines, with all the comforts of modern life about us, cannot really appreciate the enormous victory over anger, revenge, resentment, unforgiveness and fear that enabled David to soar into the pure air of God's love, to breathe its heavenly fragrance in the midst of all his sufferings. This shows that he understands the prayer relationship with God, and the delicious fruit it brings into our lives.

To rejoice in God while transcending very difficult circumstances is wonderful: "Your love is better than life itself", David says. He is here speaking about that very special quality of God that amazes us. It is His loving-kindness, the *hesed* of God, which is known and experienced by those who commune deeply with Him in prayer. When by our surrender to Him in prayer, we release God to show us His personal love, regard and care for each one of us, then we begin to understand that all life could be exchanged for one moment of His pure and holy love. Great joy is felt at the realization of His personal love for us, and praise follows naturally (see Galatians 2:20). It bubbles up from within, and may be expressed in the rejoicing of the heart, or the confession of the lips, or both. The body participates too, for we express our thankfulness to God by the lifting up of our hands as well as our hearts (v. 4).

Deep communion with God in prayer is the only thing that satiates the soul and quietens its restless longing, because it is fed at its deepest source by God, who is Spirit, and who communes with our spirit, now open to Him, so that the living waters of grace and divine life can flow freely onto the thirsty ground. The strange thing about this mystic prayer is that the deeper the soul is fed by God, the more its capacity for God increases, so that the thirst for God increases too. Therefore it cries out to God continually for more of this life-giving rain. The increased need is fed more and more by God until death removes the last obstacle to full communion, and the soul is "drowned", as it were, in the sea of God's love and mercy. This is heaven (v. 5).

When David worshipped God in the sanctuary he was aware that the golden cherubim protected the glory of God over the Ark of the Covenant, hence he saw himself, in prayer, under the shadow of those heavenly wings. For us who worship God in spirit and in truth, enjoying the mystery of the indwelling of the Trinity in our souls, we live all the time in the wonder of His presence and in the protection of His love – this is "the shadow of His wings". For David the shadow of the wings was external, but let us hope that he internalized it through his prayer. For us it is internal, yet how many of us need to walk conscious of its privilege, for this is the way to learn how to pray always and stay in the presence of God amid our daily occupations.

The person who truly loves God will not find it strange to think of Him at night. Many who love God wake up in the dark to find a chorus of praise going up to God from their hearts during sleep. Like the lover in the Song of Songs, they sleep but their heart is awake to the One they love (see Song of Songs 5:2). Those who love God like to use the quiet hours of the night to commune with Him without distraction or hindrance from the world. Worldly people whose joys are in the flesh find this inexplicable, but the heart that truly loves God cleaves to Him in all the circumstances of life. They allow God to sustain them in grace, so that they not only cope with suffering, but transcend it, and thus it can become an instrument of redemption. Suffering must be a dark and dismal experience for anyone who does not allow God to give it meaning and direction.

The last three verses of the psalm bring us back, with a jolt, to the fact that the external circumstances have not changed just because David was finding his solace in God. No. Everything remains the same. He is still being hounded by those who seek his life, and by the slanderers who aid and abet them. However, he is now able to leave all justice and retribution to God, knowing as he does that God is always on the side of the innocent and of the oppressed, and he trusts God to see justice done (see Psalm 34:6,10,15,17–20).

Just because we seek union with God in prayer, it does not follow that we shall be free of the normal injustices and persecutions that are meted out to everyone in life. Indeed those who seek God will have more than others, for they must deal with the evil they find in themselves, in others, and that opposition that comes from the Evil One himself. We concentrate on co-operating with God in eliminating the evil from ourselves, and let Him deal with others according to His justice, mercy and love, and we trust His Word in Scripture for the final defeat of the Evil One (see Revelation 20:10).

20

Psalm 88:
Prayer in Desolation

Psalm 88 is probably the saddest prayer in the Psalter. It is a lament which offers not a ray of hope or comfort, written by a man whose life was marked by suffering from his youth. It has a double title; it was composed by one of the sons of Korah, and dedicated to Heman the Ezrahite, who was the founder of the Temple choir known as the Sons of Korah, a man famed for his wisdom (see 1 Chronicles 6:33, 37, 1 Kings 4:31). It is a deeply moving testimony to the great temptation which follows an incomprehensible tragedy, when God seems deaf to prayer, leaving the sufferer to cope with naked and apparently unsupported faith.

Lord my God, I call for help by day;
I cry at night before you.
Let my prayer come into your presence.
O turn your ear to my cry.

For my soul is filled with evils;
my life is on the brink of the grave.
I am reckoned as one in the tomb:
I have reached the end of my strength
(vv. 1–4).

This sufferer, in the depths of pain, turns to God as he had done all of his life, for we die as we live. For him faith was the centre of his life, and his relationship with God the meaning of his existence, so even though God appears to have abandoned him now, he turns to prayer anyway, for God is his only source of hope and salvation. His prayer is the unremitting prayer of one who refuses to give up, either on God or on a solution to his problem. It demonstrates a very mature faith that does not need signs and wonders to support it. This is triumphant faith that can cry out across the black darkness of near despair, and refuse not to believe. It cannot fail to touch God, yet no easy answer is given. In fact the psalm gives the distinct impression that this man went to his death in this dark faith, for God asks us, in the end, to face Him as mystery and utterly other. It is the beginner in faith who needs the signs and wonders to bolster his shaky belief in the presence and love of God. The mature are treated differently; their dark faith, and fidelity to their belief that God remains loving no matter what we experience of Him, is the triumph for us and gives real glory to God.

Disregarding God's silence, the poet tells God his troubles as he has always done, and in this shows his child-like trust. He is approaching death, with no strength left. Death was a dreadful thought, because the people of his day had no revelation regarding the after-life, and so they felt that death cut them off from communion with God.

like one alone among the dead;
like the slain lying in their graves;
like those you remember no more,
cut off, as they are, from your hand.

You have laid me in the depths of the tomb,
in places that are dark, in the depths.
Your anger weighs down upon me:
I am drowned beneath your waves.

You have taken away my friends
and made me hateful in their sight.
Imprisoned, I cannot escape;
my eyes are sunken with grief.

I call to you, Lord, all the day long;
to you I stretch out my hands.
Will you work your wonders for the dead?
Will the shades stand and praise you?

Will your love be told in the grave
or your faithfulness among the dead?
Will your wonders be known in the dark
or your justice in the land of oblivion?

As for me, Lord, I call to you for help:
in the morning my prayer comes before you.
Lord, why do you reject me?
Why do you hide your face from me?

Wretched, close to death from my youth,
I have borne your trials; I am numb.
Your fury has swept down upon me;
your terrors have utterly destroyed me.

They surround me all the day like a flood,
they assail me all together.
Friend and neighbour you have taken away:
my one companion is darkness.

(vv. 5–18).

The Sons of Korah had been demoted from their Temple
duties (explained in Psalms 42–43), and they were
banished. Here this dying man fears an even greater
banishment if he is cut off from God for ever by being
thrown into the pit (v. 4). This is a more accurate translation than our "tomb" in this version. To be thrown into
the pit is to be treated like the wicked who will never see the
face of God. Imprisoned in his sickness, which is
worsening, he remembers the look of revulsion on the faces
of his friends, and knows that he has lost them too. He is

being stripped of everything he holds dear, and life itself is beginning to slip away too.

Somehow the sick man sees the hand of God in it all. He repeatedly says: "You have . . ." He sees that God has permitted that which is so crushing to him, yet his love for God is shown even in the expressions that he uses. In fact his greatest suffering is not the loss of friends, health, success or even of life; it is the loss of the presence of God, and the sense of His nearness. It is the fact that he apparently cannot get through to God in this crucial moment of his life.

From the standpoint of God's people on earth, and the worshipping community in the Temple, what is said here in verses 9–12 is true. It is on earth that God's miracles are performed, that His Word is preached, that His praise is sung, that His faithfulness is demonstrated, and, since they had no idea what happened after death, they feared they would be cut off from God. Death was seen as an enemy of all that was good (see 1 Corinthians 15:26). It was silence, inactivity, the severing of all ties with loved ones, corruption, gloom, darkness and oblivion. The psalmist got no answer from God to this dreadful dilemma. He was left with the mystery of suffering and death unanswered, for the time had not yet come for this revelation.

Even though we live in the fullness of time when Jesus overcame death in His glorious resurrection, and revealed to us that our Father has a place prepared for us in Heaven, where we will experience the joy, not only of God's presence for ever, but also the joy of our loved ones with us there, yet each of us must, at some stage in our lives, face the almost incomprehensible mystery of suffering, maybe in a lingering sickness, or in a tragedy that appears meaningless. We must face the futility of it all, and be ready to go through the "dark valley", refusing to give up on our faith and trust in God. History tells us that the saints were all tested this way to purify their faith. Witness the case of St Thérèse of Lisieux, who was so tested in her faith that

133

she felt that there was no heaven, and could only cling on in desperate hope to the revelation of Scripture and the teaching of the Church. She had to persevere in this dark faith to the moment of her death, just like the sufferer in this psalm.

Jesus has clothed our suffering and death with meaning so that we do not grieve like the unbelievers who have no hope (see 1 Thessalonians 4:13). He has conquered death and has removed its sting, which was sin (see 1 Corinthians 15:54–47). We see that He chose suffering as the most perfect way to redeem us, so we can unite our suffering, our lonliness and our darkness with His in His Passion, and so clothe our experience with redemptive meaning. For those who do not have this faith, let us lovingly bring them the light we have, to lighten their darkness.

The poor sufferer in this psalm had no idea just how greatly God would use his words of desperate faith and love. He did not know that another sufferer would be able to express His distress to His Father in exactly the same words! On the night that Jesus suffered His agony in Gethsemane, which drained Him of all strength, He was deserted by His close friends and sold by a disciple for the price of a slave. He was dragged before an unjust judge, in the person of the high priest, and accused by false witnesses, after which He was thrown into a dungeon for very dangerous prisoners to await crucifixion the following morning. This dungeon, or pit, was two floors below the house of Caiaphas, and can still be visited in Jerusalem. There, with darkness as His only companion, Jesus prayed all night to His Father, who maintained a dreadful silence during the whole Passion. Jesus was left to face the terror alone, bereft of all help. The psalm expresses His trust in God, but also His frustration at being cut off from the ministry given to Him. Through this ministry He was to reveal God's marvels to the people in His healing miracles, and also to preach the Word of God so that the people would know God's ways, and worship Him properly in spirit and in truth. He was left to face the darkness and terror of death and Hell – which is the experience of being cut off from God, so feared by the psalmist – but it was not deliverance *from* death that Jesus cried out for. It was deliverance *through* death, and it was not for Himself, but for all mankind. He had to walk through the dark corridors of death and Hell to remove its terror from us. The awesome darkness remained to the very end with Jesus too, as He cried out to His Father from the Cross the same desperate "Why?" of the psalmist. He was not spared the mystery of suffering, with its sense of futility. He had to experience it like the rest of men, but He redeemed it, gave it meaning, purpose and direction for the rest of us.

21

Psalm 91:
Protection for the Pilgrim

This psalm, written by an unknown author, is one of the most impressive testimonies in the Psalter to the inner strength experienced by the person who puts his trust in God. The poet has learned through his own intimate relationship with God, and speaks from the narrow confines of his own personal circumstances. In its present form the psalm was used in the Temple liturgy to promise the assurance of salvation, and to illustrate the wealth of blessing that flows to the individual who places his trust in God.

He who dwells in the shelter of the Most High
and abides in the shade of the Almighty
says to the Lord: "My refuge,
my stronghold, my God in whom I trust!"

It is he who will free you from the snare
of the fowler who seeks to destroy you;
he will conceal you under his pinions
and under his wings you will find refuge.

You will not fear the terror of the night
nor the arrow that flies by day,
nor the plague that prowls in the darkness
nor the scourge that lays waste at noon.

A thousand may fall at your side,
ten thousand fall at your right,
you, it will never approach;
his faithfulness is buckler and shield.

Your eyes have only to look
to see how the wicked are repaid,
you will have said: "Lord, my refuge!"
and have made the Most High your dwelling.

Upon you no evil shall fall,
no plague approach where you dwell.
For you has he commanded his angels,
to keep you in all your ways.

They shall bear you upon their hands
lest you strike your foot against a stone.
On the lion and the viper you will tread
and trample the young lion and the dragon

(vv. 1–13).

As with so many of the psalms, the first two verses give the
key to the rest of the poem. The setting is the Temple
worship, and the pilgrim is welcomed to the sanctuary. He
is reminded that if he takes shelter in God's house, putting
his trust completely in God, he will find protection. It is a
deeply personal trust that is called for, whereby the pilgrim
can relate to God as his "refuge, his fortress and his God".
If he actually trusts God in this very personal way rather
than believing in a God who is "out there somewhere" for
everybody; if he truly relies on God as on a fortress, which
is invincible, then he is already, spiritually speaking,
dwelling in the shelter of the Most High, which his physical
presence in the Temple symbolizes. To stay under God's
protection, and to abide, or live continually, in His love, is
the source of peace of mind and complete security against
all harm. This puts God in charge of one's life, which can be
lived secure in His love. The different titles given to God
here bring home to us that the person whose refuge we seek
is the God of all gods, the creator and lord of the universe,
the One who is the ultimate protection of the poor and the
weak (vv. 1–2).

137

The poet turns to us now to declare that God will rescue us also if we trust Him. We are surrounded by secret dangers, just like the hunted animal who does not realize that a pit has been dug to trap him. Because God is God He can deliver us from the things, situations or people who would prevent us from coming close to Him (v. 3).

Here in the Temple, the presence of God appeared over the Ark of the Covenant between the cherubim (see Exodus 25:22, 1 Kings 8:10–12); thus just as the mother bird protects her young by spreading her wings over them, God protects those who come to Him in trust and confidence (see Deuteronomy 32:11, Matthew 23:37). The two sides of our relationship with God are seen here in this strong, intimate and tender scene, in the powerful presence of the almighty protecting and caring for the helpless creature who rests in complete trust in His great arms (or wings). The last part of this verse is found at the end of verse 7, where it borrows images from war to show that God's faithfulness in taking care of the one entrusted to Him will destroy all opposition (v. 4).

"You will not fear" explains very simply the difference between belief and unbelief. To believe is an active reaching out to God to "take hold" of Him or His grace, which empowers us to achieve our aims. Here the power of God is used to overcome the sinister fears that attack us at night, or in the daytime. These originate either from the attack of demons, from our own troubled hearts, or even from evil persons. In each case we quickly reach the safe haven of peace by reaching out in trusting faith to God. His powerful presence comes to us to drive out all anxiety and fear, leaving us safely in His hands (vv. 5–6).

Faith soars to the heights now as the poet declares that, if you trust God for protection, you will be safe even should the world fall apart around you! He uses a picture of wartime to describe a miracle of preservation. What was impossible, humanly speaking, was within the reach of faith. St Paul makes a similar promise in Romans 8:28–35, where he tells us that everything will work out for the good for those who love God, yet the proof is only seen in the trials and persecutions suffered with total trust in God's goodness and love. The wicked, however, cannot escape the retribution due to their sins, but no evil or scourge will touch those who have taken shelter in God's love. The believers in the Temple are safe because of their relationship with God, which will provide protection for them as they return to their homes (vv. 9–10).

God's protection is given to the believers through the ministry of angels who carry out His promises of protection (see Hebrews 1:14). These angels are supernatural beings, pure spirits, who guard and protect God's children during their perilous journey through life. They reveal God's motherly solicitude for us, for they will lift us up, spiritually speaking, and carry us carefully if need be, so that we do not fall and hurt ourselves. We can go our way, therefore, in peace (vv. 11–12).

Nevertheless, childlike protectiveness and security are not the whole picture. God does not wish us to become passive about our lives. Virile strength is also given to overcome any difficulty encountered along the way. Whether the enemies are spiritual or human they can be dealt with through the power of God: Paul strikes the same note in Philippians 4:13: "There is nothing that I cannot master with the help of the One who gives me the strength." The mention of lions, adders and dragons is meant to be taken metaphorically, representing situations of grave danger which could be spiritual or natural (v. 13).

His love he set on me, so I will rescue him;
protect him for he knows my name.
When he calls I shall answer: "I am with you."
I will save him in distress and give him glory.

With length of life I will content him;
I shall let him see my saving power
(vv. 14–16).

The final verses of the psalm are the promises of God in response to the poet's faithfulness. To know God in a deeply personal intimate way is the meaning of "He knows my name". It implies a deep interior clinging to God, the involvement of authentic love. Communion with God in prayer is made easier by the continued presence of God, and the assurance of answered prayer. The promise of God's blessing covers the whole of life, material and spiritual, and includes the blessing of salvation at the end of our days. Here we see the source of the security of the God-fearing person.

Every pilgrim needs to pick up this psalm, for the lessons it teaches are essential for the spiritual journey, which as we all know is a narrow road, and a hard one (see Matthew 7:14). It is also hazardous. The whole psalm revolves around an "if" clause given in the opening verse. The many who claim to be religious may not, in fact, be living in a conscious way in the shelter of the Most High. For them, trust in God is still a doctrine which they do not experience in their everyday life. They can only say the words: "my fortress, my refuge . . ." in a theoretical way, without knowing the grace and joy of the lived reality. If they have not surrendered to God in real trust they will not rely on Him to deliver them from the hidden dangers, the anxieties or fears that threaten them. They will have to look to human solutions, for instance psychology, to understand God's miraculous deliverance of His close friends, when they cry to Him. Their tendency would be to write off such things as "luck" or coincidence, thus leaving no opening for the testimony of God's intervention in our daily lives.

The truly spiritual pilgrim knows differently because he has learned to cling to God in real surrender and trust. He has many tales to relate of God's deliverance from all kinds of dangers, both perils from within, originating in his own sinfulness, and those whose source comes from the weaknesses of others. He fears no evil because he relies on the might of God, whose presence and power are there to save him day and night. And so he learns to walk in complete peace, because he trusts God's promise that everything will work out for the best in the end.

One of the treacherous points of the journey is illustrated in Matthew and Luke, where we see Jesus in the wilderness in fasting and prayer, seeking His Father's will for His ministry. He was approached by the Evil One, who, to put Him off His journey, misquoted this psalm, saying that the angels would save Him from harm if He jumped from the pinnacle of the Temple. Such a jump would certainly kill him. God's promise in the psalm does not cover tempting providence by rash behaviour. Insight was needed by Jesus then, and by us now, to see through the deceptive offer to the real message, which was a suggestion to him to commit suicide. Jesus stayed in obedience and surrender to God's will, while exposing the devil with a correct quotation from Scripture: that he should not put God to the test (see Deuteronomy 6:16). St Mark tells us that the angels did minister to Jesus at this point, but it was because He stayed under the shelter of the Most High (see Matthew and Luke 4, Mark 1:13).

Remaining in an attitude of surrender to God's will enables us to move into the power and authority which Jesus gave us to ". . . tread underfoot serpents and scorpions and the whole strength of the enemy; nothing will ever harm you" (Luke 10:19; J.B.). The pilgrim can, therefore, continue his journey protected by his faith and trust in God. He also has God's presence always and the Scriptures to defend him in time of need. This is part of the spiritual armour, described by Paul in Ephesians 6:10–20, which we need in order to persevere in the spiritual warfare involved on the journey.

22

Psalm 95:
Encounter with God

From primitive times the Church has used this psalm as a call to worship. It was known as the *Venite* from the Latin for "O come!" It is still used as the invitatory psalm for morning prayer in the Roman Breviary. Its austere conclusion balances the exuberance of the opening verses with the same realism that the ancient prophets portrayed, when they called for great and fine deeds to follow great and fine words of praise.

The authorship is unknown, but Hebrews 4:7 ascribes it to David, probably because the whole Psalter was ascribed to him as its most celebrated author. The psalm appears to have been used for the Feast of Tabernacles, an autumn festival when the people relived, in token, their time and encampment in the wilderness. This psalm was part of a liturgy which looked upon God as lord of the universe, and who now, as the reigning monarch, was surveying His people, and reviewing the Covenant He had with them. The psalm has two parts: verses 1–7a, containing a hymn to prepare the people for their encounter with God; and verses 7b–11, comprising a warning from God that obedience to His Law and His Word was more important than anything else.

> Come, ring out our joy to the Lord;
> hail the rock who saves us.
> Let us come before him, giving thanks,
> with songs let us hail the Lord.

A mighty God is the Lord,
a great king above all gods.
In his hands are the depths of the earth;
the heights of the mountains are his.
To him belongs the sea, for he made it
and the dry land shaped by his hands.

Come in; let us bow and bend low;
let us kneel before the God who made us
for he is our God and we
the people who belong to his pasture,
the flock that is led by his hand.

O that today you would listen to his voice!
"Harden not your hearts as at Meribah,
as on that day at Massah in the desert
when your fathers put me to the test;
when they tried me, though they saw my work.

For forty years I was wearied of these people
and I said: 'Their hearts are astray,
these people do not know my ways.'
Then I took an oath in my anger:
'Never shall they enter my rest'"

(vv. 1–11).

We are invited to come singing into the presence of God; to come with enthusiastic joy and thanksgiving as the best way to express our love to God, who is both saviour and king. We are encouraged to give an acclamation that is worthy of Him, instead of drifting into His presence apathetic and preoccupied, and therefore unaware of our obligation to offer praise and thanks, and unable to enter into deep communion with Him. The "Rock" who saves us is a reference either to the rock that gushed forth with water in the wilderness, or to the rock on which the Temple was built; perhaps to both. In either case God is the author of

143

our salvation (see Exodus 17:1–2, Deuteronomy 32:4) (vv. 1–2).

The reason why we should come singing and rejoicing is now given to us. It is because we become aware of who God really is. As creator of the universe, the Lord has pre-eminence over all other so-called gods. He is the mighty ruler, whose hands hold both "heights" and "depths", the sea and the dry land. According to popular belief at the time, the depths of the underworld were the realm of evil powers, and the heights of the mountains the abode of the gods (see Amos 9:2, Psalms 6:5, 30:9, 88:10–11, etc). The Lord God transcends all of these "nothings". Everything that exists comes from Him and is ruled by Him, who is supreme Lord.

In the New Testament Paul took up this theme to de-monstrate the supremacy of Christ over all "thrones, dominations, sovereignties and powers" which were created through and for the Son of God. Every power, whether in Heaven, on earth or in the underworld, must submit to Him (see Colossians 1:16, Philippians 2:10, Romans 8:38f). None of these powers can separate us from God's loving care and protection. Indeed the miracle of our incorporation into Christ means that the whole world is ours, for we belong to Christ, who belongs to God (see 1 Corinthians 3:23). This vast and varied world of ours is both hand-made by our loving God, and hand-held by Him too (vv. 3–5).

Consequently the praise and thanksgiving of every creature is His due, as is our humble submission to Him. Hence true worship entails prostrating oneself in His au-gust presence. Without this reverential awe the opening jubilation is but empty noise and self-indulgence, in the enjoyment of ritual and communal singing. This is not the worship of strangers coming out of fear, but that of God's own people, redeemed by His own hand, a people who come to Him with confidence and love, calling Him our maker, and our God, because He is the shepherd who cares for us and pastures us like a flock of sheep, a people whom He Himself guides (vv. 6–7).

Old Testament piety had a profound concern for inner truthfulness, shown by the fact that the sentiments of praise and worship were considered legitimate only if followed by a readiness to obey God's Word and keep His commandments. Both Old and New Testaments present us with obedience to God's Word as the acceptable sign of love to God. To "listen" to the Lord, to "hear" His voice, and to "hearken" to His Word all express the need to respond to God's Word with the inner submission of the heart. Procrastination is not accepted: the presence of God is here today, and the response must be given today also. The choice is put before us again to become more committed to the Lord or to back-slide down the slippery slope to join the wicked, who refuse to listen to the Lord or obey His Word.

We are now reminded of the need to learn from history so that we shall not repeat its mistakes. Massah and Meribah were two places in the wilderness where the people of Israel rebelled against God, refusing either to listen to His Word or obey it. The names mean "dispute" and "testing, or temptation", and they sum up the sour sceptical spirit of the desert pilgrims during the crisis at Rephidim (see Exodus 17:1–7), and the final one at Kadesh, which cost Moses the Promised Land (see Numbers 20:1–13). The emphasis is on their refusal to take God at His Word, even though they had experienced His presence and His wonders in the Exodus, and during their trek through the wilderness. To use human language, God was disgusted with their refusal to learn from Him the way of peace and salvation which would lead to their fulfilment. Because of their rebellion He left them to experience the restless strife of their erring hearts, which resulted in their wandering aimlessly for forty years without most of that generation ever seeing the Promised Land. God's anger here is His sense of outrage that the people would be so stupid as to prevent their own happiness and fulfilment, which He alone could give them – and was willing to give them! So they did not enter "my rest", meaning that they did not experience the joy, peace and security of the Promised Land (vv. 8–11).

This warning, given during the Feast of Tabernacles, when the people were in festive mood, and probably romanticizing the experience of their forefathers in the desert, is a cold douche of realism to prevent them from having a liturgy devoid of historical truth. It is another reminder that God is more interested in our character than in our comfort, and that the true aim of liturgy is to help us on the journey of salvation, not to entertain us with beauty and ritual.

This Psalm is expounded for us by the author of the Letter to the Hebrews in 3:7–4:11. Here we see yet again that the psalms carry a deeper message than even the original human author may have suspected, but a meaning that the divine author, the Holy Spirit, obviously intended, since it is given to us in another inspired text. Addressing himself to Christians now, the author says that this text refers to us (Hebrews 3:7) when it speaks of the obligation to obey God's will and God's Word. He expands the today of the psalm to the whole Christian era, for with God a thousand years is like a single day (Psalm 90:4). Each day of our lives God is present to us with His grace, present in our own hearts, present in His Word, present in the Eucharist, in prayer, and when the body of Christians meet together. Our choice is to listen for His guidance and obey, or to harden our hearts in disobedience. He reminds us that the people who rebelled against God in the wilderness were not the pagans and unbelievers in Egypt, but God's own people who had willingly accepted the Covenant on Sinai, and who had experienced all His loving care. It is a timely warning to us who have experienced the wonder of Redemption through Christ, and who bask in our glory as the redeemed community of the New Testament. It is possible for us, too, to lose our way and miss out on the promised rest God offers us in union with Jesus, that fullness of peace, joy and security Jesus promised to those who keep His commandments (see John 14:27, 15:11).

St Augustine understood this promised rest when he said that our hearts are restless until they rest in God. If we refuse to listen to and obey God's Word, we condemn ourselves to wander through the wilderness of this life, with our personal problems unsolved, never discovering the true meaning of life, and perhaps never finding the way of peace. This self-inflicted punishment is so unnecessary that it grieves the Holy Spirit who indwells us. We are reminded, too, of Jesus weeping over Jerusalem at the end of His ministry because she refused to listen to her saviour and learn from Him the way of peace – therefore she could not be protected from the punishment that would follow her choice (see Luke 19:42–44).

23

Psalm 96:
The Lord Reigns

The background of this psalm, whose author is unknown, is the triumphal entry of the Ark into Jerusalem for the first time (see 1 Chronicles 16:23–33). King David arranged for the Ark to be taken to Jerusalem with great pomp and ceremony. God's throne is now firmly fixed among His people, and they exult with joyful songs of praise to Him.

O sing a new song to the Lord,
sing to the Lord all the earth.
O sing to the Lord, bless his name.

Proclaim his help day by day,
tell among the nations his glory
and his wonders among all the peoples.

The Lord is great and worthy of praise,
to be feared above all gods;
the gods of the heathens are naught.

It was the Lord who made the heavens,
his are majesty and state and power
and splendour in his holy place.

Give the Lord, you families of peoples,
give the Lord glory and power,
give the Lord the glory of his name.

Bring an offering and enter his courts,
worship the Lord in his temple.
O earth, tremble before him.

Proclaim to the nations: "God is King."
The world he made firm in its place;
he will judge the peoples in fairness.

Let the heavens rejoice and earth be glad,
let the sea and all within it thunder praise,
let the land and all it bears rejoice,
all the trees of the wood shout for joy

at the presence of the Lord for he comes,
he comes to rule the earth.
With justice he will rule the world,
he will judge the peoples with his truth
(vv. 1–13).

The build-up of the repeated words "sing . . . O sing . . . proclaim" at the opening of the psalm illustrate the vigour of the people's praise to God, and the almost irrepressible excitement at the prospect of the Lord's arrival in their midst. When He comes He will find a community of praise and worship awaiting Him, as is His due. True praise to God is always a "new" song, for it comes from a loving heart responding in gratitude to Him for the wonders of salvation. It is always expressed with real feeling to match the freshness of God's mercies, which are new every morning. Real praise also includes "all the earth" for we are aware of our unity with all creation. Praise is a proclamation of God's glory, not in the sense of missionary activity, but of speaking out into all creation, and of joining with all others who praise God. This includes the animal and plant kingdoms, who praise God by their lives (vv. 1– 3).

Only the true God, who is creator and Lord of the universe is worthy of our loving praise and our reverential awe. All the idols worshipped by the heathens are worthless. This was a great challenge to the ideas accepted among the peoples of that time. It is also a challenge to the people of our day, not to give their time and attention to worthless materialism, and to the false cults that are rampant. The psalmist stops short of saying that the idols do not exist and are nothing in the true sense. The many people today who are caught on the treadmill of false cults likewise do not realize that their "nothing" is going nowhere! They are involved in a cult which has no worth, no value for time or eternity. Only the true worship of God in spirit and in truth has value; only the true worshippers realize the majesty and glory of God revealed in His sanctuary. The earthly sanctuary was a copy of the heavenly one revealed by God Himself; its true worship was a preparation for the full revelation of redemption in and through Christ, who, as the true Temple of God, surpassed in glory and dignity the old sanctuary (see Hebrews 8:5, John 1:14, 2:21) (vv. 4–6).

The threefold "sing" at the beginning of the psalm is now replaced by a threefold "give to the Lord". It is not enough to sing and dance to the Lord. The worshippers must also bring gifts humbly to Him in reverential awe and fear, thus acknowledging His splendour and majesty. There is another reminder that all nations must so worship God, even though all true worship is given in the name of all peoples on the earth. This is an acknowledgement of the essential oneness of all mankind (vv. 7–9).

Reaching the climax of the psalm, we see the people respond to God's presence with a combination of reverential fear and rapturous joy, which shows how deeply moved they were by the manifest greatness of God. They declare that God reigns over all the earth. Men may feel totally secure under His benign and just rule, where everyone is treated fairly, and God reveals His triumphant justice in His plan of salvation. God has everything under control, as everything in heaven and on earth comes under His righteous rule. And so we reach the ecstatic climax of the psalm, and also the central verse of the Psalter, when the people cry out to the heavens and the earth, to the sea and all it contains, to all plant life on earth, to thunder praise to God, and shout for joy. The cause of this great rejoicing is the coming of God's Kingdom on earth, when God will reign as king, and the earth, at last, will have a just peace.

The prophetic message of this psalm should not be lost. The day eventually came for Israel, for the Church and the world, when the incarnate God, in the person of Jesus Christ, rode triumphantly into Jerusalem amid the joyful acclaim of the people. He took His throne in the Temple of God, declaring it to be His Father's house (see John 1:13–25). The glory of God was now fully manifested in their midst, if only they had eyes to see. The glory was no longer hidden behind the veil in the Holy of Holies; it was right here in their midst, and they could touch Him, but none of them realized at that time that Jesus was the new Temple; that He was the Holy of Holies; that God was no longer distant from His people, for they all had access to His august majesty in the person of their mediator, Jesus, the Messiah. But they were blind, and most of them missed the glory of Israel after having waited thousands of years for it. When He came He was too ordinary! The problem with most of God's people is that they have not penetrated the mystery of the incarnation, and so they miss the significance of everything that God offers to them. How sad!

As the glory of Israel rode into Jerusalem on a donkey, in the same humble way that the Ark had entered Jerusalem so many years before, Jesus told the leaders that if they stopped the people from giving their due glory and praise to God the very stones would cry out, because all creation was waiting for the Son of God to manifest Himself, and begin the release of the world from its landslide into decadence (see Luke 19:39–40, Romans 8:21f). The reason for His coming was to establish the Kingdom of God on earth, to initiate God's rule over the nations. One day He will return amid the jubilant joy and celebration of His people to bring

151

the final fulfilment of all God's promises. Then He shall reign for ever as king of kings and lord of lords, surrounded by a chosen race, a people set apart to sing the praises of God in joyful thanksgiving (see 1 Peter 2:9).

24

Psalm 103:
In Praise of God's Love

Psalm 103, which is attributed to King David, is one of the finest fruits of biblical faith. Combined with its neighbour, Psalm 104, we have two psalms that praise God as saviour and creator, father and sustainer. One who is both merciful and mighty. Together they illustrate two aspects of our prayer and praise, namely, that the beloved *Abba*, "Daddy", whom we love and adore, is also the great author and ruler of the universe. This produces both love and humble, adoring reverence in us. Our *Abba* is the king of the universe.

> My soul, give thanks to the Lord,
> all my being, bless his holy name.
> My soul, give thanks to the Lord
> and never forget all his blessings.

> It is he who forgives all your guilt,
> who heals every one of your ills,
> who redeems your life from the grave,
> who crowns you with love and compassion,
> who fills your life with good things,
> renewing your youth like an eagle's
>
> (vv. 1–5).

The psalmist shows us how to shake off apathy, worldliness and gloom in order to enter the presence of God in prayer. This is not a choirmaster urging his congregation to enter into praise and worship; it is David speaking to his own soul, calling upon himself to praise God with thanksgiving. It expresses his desire to hearken to the voice of the Lord, both in the Scriptures – as we shall see in verse 6 – and in the intimacy of prayer. He is aware of the need to create a "sacred space" or a divine atmosphere for communion with God. Then, face to face with God, in faith, he can enjoy the living and loving presence of *Abba*-God.

David wants to be present to God with his whole being, because the true relationship with God is expressed in the command to love God "with your whole heart. . . your whole soul . . . and your whole being" (see Deuteronomy 6:4–5, Matthew 22:37–40). Nothing but complete presence and surrender in faith on the part of the person praying is worthy of the loving presence of the saving God. While approaching God's Holiness with reverential awe, we give ourselves up to His loving embrace.

David then arouses his soul to thanksgiving by using his memory to recall the manifold goodness of God towards him throughout his life. Counting our blessings is an important exercise; we arouse our gratitude to God, but we also prevent ourselves from taking life for granted and thus blunting our response to it. Everything comes to us from the hand of the good God. It is merely truth to acknowledge it (vv. 1–3).

The poet, now more responsive to God, begins to look at the abundance of God's blessings in his life. His reflection enables him to recognize that the light, life and presence of God has pervaded his whole life, bringing with it deliverance from sickness and death. The forgiveness of sin is the beginning of real liberation. The healing of the body is secondary to this; it is only a foretaste of the full redemption of our bodies promised later (see Romans 8:23). The final liberation is from the pit of Hell (see John 3:16, 5:25, 28, etc). No life can prosper when the cancer of sin rules it, and left unchecked it leads to death in the real sense, namely, the absence of God, which *is* Hell (vv. 3–5).

The Lord does deeds of justice,
gives judgement for all who are oppressed.
He made known his ways to Moses
and his deeds to Israel's sons.

The Lord is compassion and love,
slow to anger and rich in mercy.
His wrath will come to an end;
he will not be angry for ever.
He does not treat us according to our sins
nor repay us according to our faults.

For as the heavens are high above the earth
so strong is his love for those who fear him.
As far as the east is from the west
so far does he remove our sins.

As a father has compassion on his sons,
the Lord has pity on those who fear him;
for he knows of what we are made,
he remembers that we are dust

                    (vv. 6–14).

Looking back in history to the events of the Exodus, David tries to learn its lessons. The Exodus tale is an extraordinary testimony to God's grace, and unmerited favour, in the context of man's unworthiness and ingratitude; to the forgiving, healing and saving grace of God that David sang about in the opening verses. Besides, Exodus is also the record of God's righteousness. God is just and right in all that He does, and is always on the side of the oppressed, no matter who the oppressor is. David learned this to his cost in his woeful relationships with Uriah and Bathsheba. There David was the oppressor, and He found that God still defended the weak, this time against David himself. If all of God's deeds can be summed up in His righteousness, and His goodness to us, then we can have hope for the future, for the history of mankind is a complex of God's actions and man's response to them. The darker side of history is entirely man's doing.

God revealed His ways to Moses (see Exodus 33:13). He allowed His intentions and His will to be known in a series of gracious acts that invited Israel into intimacy with Himself. God's self-revelation to Moses in Exodus 32 is referred to here by David. There God allowed Himself to be seen as tender and compassionate in the wake of the apostasy of the Golden Calf. Both here and elsewhere He showed that He never treats us as our sins deserve. Strict justice from God would be the worst thing any sinner could receive! God always tempers justice with mercy, because He does not desire the death of the sinner, rather that he be converted and live (see Ezekiel 18:32, John 8:1–11).

How do we describe this wonderful love of God towards us? It cannot be measured in human terms, for it is impossible for man to squeeze God's love and inconceivable majesty and greatness into any scheme of ours. Man is good at meting out retribution to his fellow man – "an eye for an eye and a tooth for a tooth" – but God's ways are infinitely different, and His compassion for the innate sinfulness of His creatures is utterly awesome. These words from Isaiah 55:6–9 express the same message: "Seek the Lord while He may be found, call on Him while He is near. Let the wicked abandon his way, the evil man his thoughts. Let him turn back to the Lord who will take pity on him, to our God who is rich in forgiving; for my thoughts are not your thoughts, my ways not your ways – it is the Lord who speaks. Yes, the heavens are as high above the earth as my ways are above your ways, my thoughts above your thoughts" (J.B. – I have substituted "The Lord" for Yahweh).

To illustrate God's incomparable grace, David now resorts to the lovely image of father and child. God is a father to us, not just a ruler and judge. As father He has inexpressible tenderness and patience with His children as they grow to maturity. What spoils the relationship with Him for us is our own fear, born of sin and infidelity to His grace, for we compare Him with men and their retribution. We forget that God is aware that we are made of dust, and that therefore we are capable of very little in the spiritual sense. If we were more conscious of this fact we would rely more on His grace and mercy. Jesus reminded us of this in John 15:5 when He said that apart from Him we could do nothing. The other side of the coin was given to us by St Paul in Philippians 4:13, where he claimed that there was nothing that we could not master with the help of the One who gives us strength (vv. 6–14).

> As for man, his days are like grass;
> he flowers like the flower of the field;
> the wind blows and he is gone
> and his place never sees him again.
>
> But the love of the Lord is everlasting
> upon those who hold him in fear;
> his justice reaches out to children's children
> when they keep his covenant in truth,
> when they keep his will in their mind.
>
> The Lord has set his sway in heaven
> and his kingdom is ruling over all.
> Give thanks to the Lord, all his angels,
> mighty in power, fulfilling his word,
> who heed the voice of his word.
>
> Give thanks to the Lord, all his hosts,
> his servants who do his will.
> Give thanks to the Lord, all his works,
> in every place where he rules.
> My soul, give thanks to the Lord!
>
> (vv. 15–22).

We are so insignificant that the span of our lives can be compared to that of the grass, here today and gone tomorrow. Yet we "strut and fret our hour upon the stage" as if we were very important! As the flowers cannot survive without sunshine, so neither can we without God's compassion. The miracle of God's love is such that it pervades our lives. He is the life of our life, as well as being the love of our love. God's love is our life. Without it we die. Using the same image of the grass of the field to explain the shortness of our lives, Jesus begged us to trust the Father's loving care for us instead of worrying about things we could not solve anyway (see Matthew 6:25–34). The real glory of this "dust", this "nothing" that is us, is the fact that God has made us His children, and destined us for eternal happiness with Him (vv. 15–18).

It is strange to observe that when man stands tall in his pride and arrogance he sees nothing of the glory of God. He is blinded. But when he humbles himself into his native dust, vision is granted him, and he not only can behold the glory of God, but also the wonder of all creation in a universe that vibrates with the presence and glory of Heaven. He can now appreciate that God is not only the father of mankind, but also ruler of the universe, and that he deserves more praise than an infinite number of worlds, full of saints, could give Him. So David now calls upon the angelic choirs to praise God for us and with us. But all creation must join them too, including the plant and animal kingdoms who are part of God's empire. None of this has value if the poet himself, and we who read his prayer, do not join them. The psalm ends as it began.

25

Psalm 113:
Who is Like the Lord our God?

This psalm belongs to the Hallel collection of the Psalter, comprising Psalms 113–118; their authorship is unknown. They were used in the Jewish liturgy for the great feasts, like Passover and Pentecost. At the family celebration of Passover Psalms 113 and 114 were sung before the meal, while Psalms 115–118 were sung afterwards. These were, therefore, the last psalms prayed by Jesus before His Passion (see Matthew 26:26, 30, Mark 14:22, 26). This psalm is a hymn of praise to God, who is both glorious and compassionate.

Alleluia!
Praise, O servants of the Lord,
praise the name of the Lord!
May the name of the Lord be blessed
both now and for evermore!
From the rising of the sun to its setting
praised be the name of the Lord!

High above all nations is the Lord,
above the heavens his glory.
Who is like the Lord, our God,
who has risen on high to his throne
yet stoops from the heights to look down,
to look down upon heaven and earth?

From the dust he lifts up the lowly,
from the dungheap he raises the poor
to set him in the company of princes,
yes, with the princes of his people.
To the childless wife he gives a home
and gladdens her heart with children

(vv. 1–9).

This psalm opens with the liturgical shout: Halleluia! This is a command to praise the Lord, an exuberant expression of faith in God. The worshippers at the celebration are called "servants of the Lord", which is both an apt title for them and an honour, for all the great men of old whom God used were called God's servants; so it sets them in the royal line from Abraham and the Patriarchs down through Moses, to those present in the Temple for this feast. This command to God's servants to render Him praise is both a recognition of their duty to obey God's commandments, and an expression of their joyous privilege of living in permanent relationship with Him. Praise is the loving homage of committed disciples to the One who has revealed Himself as their Lord and father.

The worshipping congregation is aware that they are not alone, for they immediately become aware of participating in the vast paean of praise ascending to God from all creation, throughout the expanse of all time and all generations. Praise therefore lifts us out of our limited awareness of ourselves into a sense of oneness with all creation. It also lifts the heart to Heaven, making us aware of, and indeed enter into, the praise of the angelic spirits who offer their worship to God continuously (see Revelation 5:6–14).

The spiritual basis for praise is God's transcendent glory. God is sovereign Lord of the universe, and Lord of history, and so there can be no one like Him. He is the exalted ruler of all nations and kingdoms, whose home is far above the heavens. Therefore He is "wholly other", unique and perfect in His own being, needing neither authority nor power from His creatures on earth (see John 18:36–37). The psalmist's statement, which re-echoes the song of Moses at the Red Sea (see Exodus 15:11), shows that God cannot be compared with anything on the earth. His glory transcends anything that can be known or understood by creatures. St Paul underlined this when he said that no eye could see, nor ear hear nor heart understand what God has prepared, in heaven, for those who love Him, and this was merely a description of heaven, not of God Himself! He is indescribable. God cannot be grasped by the human intellect, but He can be experienced by those who love Him, so that they somehow understand experientially what can never be understood intellectually (see Ephesians 3:14–21).

The extraordinary thing about this great transcendent God is that He does not stay aloof in heaven. Instead He stoops down to earth to bridge the gap that separates creatures from Him. He reveals Himself to us by His Word, His prophets, His covenants, and His promises through His saints. Above all He revealed Himself fully in ultimate humility and love through the incarnation of His only begotten Son, Jesus, who came to be the bridge that connected God and man, heaven and earth (see Genesis 28:10–17, John 1:51). When we praise God, we do so through Jesus, our bridge, also with Him as our brother, and in Him because of our oneness with Him. The ultimate act of graciousness on God's part was when Jesus "stooped down" for us in His Passion and death to pay the terrible price to become the bridge of salvation for the whole world. This is the cause of our ceaseless praise and thanksgiving to God.

The greatness of God's mercy and love are best seen against the background of our nothingness, when we realize that He stoops down to mere dust. Not only does He stoop down from His glorious throne to reach His creatures, but He longs to reach those who suffer most. He

161

is not looking for anything from us save a response of love for love, the surrender of our heart in response to the giving of His; and this is all we have to give. He reaches down to us in order to lift us up to Him, to make us participators in the divine nature, children by adoption and co-heirs with His only begotten Son. There is no greater way he can glorify His creature than this! (see 1 Samuel 2:8, 1 Kings 16:2, 1 Corinthians 1:27–31).

The poet is basing these verses on the story of Hannah in 1 Samuel 1:1–2:21. Childlessness was considered a disgrace in her day; a husband could banish a woman from the home, or could lessen her rights or privileges and make her life unbearable, whereas the mother of children was protected by the law from unfair dismissal. Thus we see that God cares for the most distressed and humiliated among His children. Hannah's joy in experiencing God's mercy was shared by all Israel, partly because God gave her one of Israel's greatest prophets in her son Samuel. Her prayer had been answered out of all proportion to her request (see Ephesians 3:21). Hannah's magnificat has been sung ever since in praise to God.

Great though it was, it cannot be compared to the joy of Mary of Nazareth, when God Himself, in the person of Jesus, stooped down from His throne of glory to take up His abode in her in the incarnation, making her not only the fulfilment of the Ark of the Covenant – although surpassing it in glory – but also the mother of God Himself. This was the ultimate act of love on God's part to His creatures, and the most incredible election of a human being that could ever be contemplated. The Ark of the Covenant merely held a sign of God's Word in the stone tablets, and a sign of God's bread in the manna, and a symbol of the priesthood in Aaron's rod; the manifestation of God's Glory was outside it. Mary, on the other hand, held Jesus within her, He who was the Word of God, the manna, and the great high priest all in one great mystery. Mary's joy, and Mary's magnificat, is shared by the whole world, for it was not just a prophet who was given to her but the Messiah Himself. Each generation continues to sing her song of praise to God, even those who do not fully understand or accept the mystery she holds. She joins Hannah in telling us that God shares His greatest secrets with "little ones", those people who are not great in their own eyes, and whose humility and purity enable them to enter very deeply into the mystery of God. To this wonderful woman God entrusted, not only Jesus His Son, but also the whole Church that she would be the spiritual mother of all His adopted children, whether they acknowledged her or not. She has been enthroned in God's house, therefore, as queen and mother of all His children (see Luke 1:26–55, John 19:26–27).

26

Psalm 121:
The Pilgrim Song

This song, of unknown authorship, belongs to a group of psalms called the Songs of Ascent, or in popular language, the Book of Pilgrim Songs, which include Psalms 120–134. It is a prayer of quiet assurance of God's love, and trust in Him, by a pilgrim setting out on a perilous journey to Jerusalem to celebrate the Lord's festival.

I lift up my eyes to the mountains:
from where shall come my help?
My help shall come from the Lord
who made heaven and earth.

May he never allow you to stumble!
Let him sleep not, your guard.
No, he sleeps not nor slumbers,
Israel's guard.

The Lord is your guard and your shade;
at your right hand he stands.
By day the sun shall not smite you
nor the moon in the night.

The Lord will guard you from evil,
he will guard your soul.
The Lord will guard your going and coming
both now and for ever

(vv. 1–8).

Setting out on this perilous journey through the mountains which were the domain of robbers, wild beasts and unknown terrors, the pilgrim looks about and anxiously enquires where he can look for help in the dread and insecurity that he will experience on the way. Suddenly he looks beyond the hills to the heavens and realizes that his beloved maker and master is Lord of the universe. It is the Lord Himself who is his security. The only person who can really help is He who transcends everything, the One who is over all yet within all. The mighty God thinks it is not beneath Him to reach down from Heaven to help His child in need. This knowledge releases all anxiety and doubt, so that the pilgrim can continue his journey joyfully and trustingly (vv. 1–2).

This poem reads like a dialogue between the pilgrim and perhaps his wife, who is staying at home, expressing her anxiety that nothing will happen to him on the trip. But the anxiety is immediately replaced by loving confidence in God who keeps eternal vigil over His children, and especially over His chosen people. Beyond this simple affirmation of faith is the wonderful thought that the creator-God is neither dormant nor passive towards His creatures. He is a living God who maintains a living relationship with His children, which has here-and-now practical results in our lives. Reflection on the history of Israel affirms that God, the good shepherd, really cares for His flock in a practical way. The lovely part of it is that this pilgrim knows how to reach out to this loving God and claim for himself the protection he knows that God gives to the nation as a whole (vv. 3–4).

At last we reach the full assurance of triumphant faith. The statements are all positive now. There is no anxiety or doubt left. The Lord protects you and shades you from the terrible heat of the sun. He is there at your right hand in all situations and decision making, so that no harm will come to you, day or night. The mention of the moon as a problem indicates a popular belief at the time that it was the source of some illnesses. God's presence with the pilgrim was his protection from known and unknown dangers. With God on his side everything would turn out for the good (sec Romans 8:31) (vv. 5–6).

Here the psalm breaks out from its concentration on the individual and the immediate to cover the whole of existence. God's protection does not guarantee us a cushioned, carefree existence, but a well-armed one. Compare this with Psalm 23:4, which tells us that in going through the dark valley we are protected by God. In neither case are we told that God brings us by a route that has no dangers. As we read in John 17, we are not taken from the world as it is, but we are protected from the Evil One, and from all danger, when we allow God to be our protector. The encouraging promise here is that the Lord does protect your life. This is a many-sided reality, which includes both your physical life, but more importantly the inner life of the soul. Jesus clarified this promise when He said that not a hair of your head would perish (see Luke 21:18); He gave this assurance for the time of persecution, when we would need it most.

God's protection covers not only the journeys we make in life, but more importantly the journey of life itself. In our perilous pilgrimage through life to find the Promised Land, or the place of rest in God, we face many known and unknown dangers. Some originate within ourselves, some from without, but God is with us all the way, so we have nothing to fear, for we shall reach our journey's end safely in the New Jerusalem, where we shall celebrate the Lord's festival for ever. Jesus promised to be with us on all the days that were coming, even to the very end (see Matthew 28:20), not only for the individual but also for the Church on her pilgrim journey through history. The Lord is with her, and the gates of Hell will never prevail, even though the Church will have to go through many dark valleys before that great day of her reunion with her bridegroom, and the final Messianic banquet in heaven.

Whether for the individual or for the Church as a whole, our greatest joy, and our greatest boast, is that the Lord is with us all the way, not because we deserve such a privilege, but because of His great loving-kindness.

27

Psalm 123:
All Eyes on Jesus!

This very simple prayer also comes from the collection of
pilgrim songs. The nation of Israel, in the person of this
pilgrim, expresses her grief over foreign domination in
post-exilic times (probably the overlordship of Persia), but
there were also pressures and problems within the nation
itself. What makes this poem great is the solution it offers
to both the individual and the nation to find its peace in
God. It offers illuminating help to anyone who wants to
walk close to the Lord also.

> To you have I lifted up my eyes,
> you who dwell in the heavens:
> my eyes, like the eyes of slaves
> on the hand of their lords.
>
> Like the eyes of a servant
> on the hand of her mistress,
> so our eyes are on the Lord our God
> till he show us his mercy.
>
> Have mercy on us, Lord, have mercy.
> We are filled with contempt.
> Indeed all too full is our soul
> with the scorn of the rich,
> (with the proud man's disdain)
> (vv. 1–4).

Like the traveller in Psalm 121, this sufferer knows God,
and therefore he unerringly finds victory, even though he is

in more difficult circumstances. The solution is the same, but the spiritual victory is greater. Like St Paul he could say: "I know the One in whom I believe" (see 2 Timothy 1:12). In his distress he confidently lifts up his eyes to heaven, thus putting his problem in a context large enough for it to be solved. In troubled times our choice is to magnify the problem or magnify the Lord! When placed in the hands of the infinite One, the problem loses its power to frighten or to freeze us into inactivity. Jesus began the Lord's Prayer by putting it into the same vast context of the Father in heaven. He expected us to deal with all our life problems through this relationship with the father of man-kind.

Aware of the immense difference between the awesome majesty and splendour of God on the one hand, and the lowliness and helplessness of the creature on the other, the pilgrim approaches God humbly and with submission, just as slaves approached the masters of their day. There is a poignancy here because this pilgrim could possibly have served his time, like the rest of the nation, in long years of slavery, and learned the hard way that pride and stubbornness merely worked to his own destruction, whereas humility and submission were the only way to survive. He now transposes this knowledge into his rela-tionship with God, because God, after all, was seen as the great ruler of the universe. If he had to come trembling into the presence of mere human masters who were not even kings, then how much reverence would be required of one who dared to enter the presence of the King of Kings?

The relationship with God is described in the utter attentiveness of the slave-girl to her mistress, and the slave-boy to his master. The poet is not saying that God is cruel, like many of the masters and mistresses of the day, who were ready to punish at any moment. Rather he expresses the reverential awe of the creature before the creator, and the utter dependence of the creature on God's mercy and goodness, whilst acknowledging God's absolute power and lordship over the world and submitting to Him in everything. The difference lies in the fact that God is not only supreme Lord, but also the *Pater familias*, the father of Israel, or, in the words of St Paul, the father from whom every family, whether spiritual or natural, takes its name (see Ephesians 3:14–15). We are utterly dependent on this kind and generous Father for all our spiritual and temporal needs. This image also implies that the pilgrim, and the nation as a whole, refuse to ease the strain of waiting on God by renouncing Him, or to buy off the contempt of the unbelievers by joining them. They will wait in confident love for the Father to notice their plight, and supply their need.

Jesus used the ideas expressed in this psalm to urge the Church to remain faithful, and to watch for His return in the Second Coming. He said that He expects to find His servants at their employment. Those who prove unfaithful and therefore unworthy of such a master will be punished (see Matthew 24:45–51). He expressed a similar idea in the waiting of the wise and foolish virgins for the bridegroom to return. Only those who were ready, and actively waiting, entered the banquet. In the parable of the talents each of the servants is gifted for his task and will be judged on his use of those gifts (see Matthew 25:1–30). Clearly the devotion of the slave-boy to his master or the slave-girl to her mistress urges upon us real devotion to the accomplishment of God's will in our lives.

The humility and submission of the pilgrim provide the background to the lovely petition to God to be gracious, and to manifest, yet again, His loving-kindness to His people. The very simplicity of the request reveals the depth of prayer in the heart of this man, and is a reminder of Jesus' teaching that we would not be heard for our many words (see Matthew 6:7–8). The pilgrim makes this request because he and the nation are suffering from the proud arrogance and contempt of their oppressors. It is only when this suffering is highlighted at the end of the psalm that we appreciate the purity and restrained but loving surrender that enabled this afflicted man to lift his eyes above all the oppressive darkness surrounding him, to breathe the pure air of God's love and life as he seeks redemption and peace for himself and for the nation.

This psalm gives eloquent guidance for the spiritual pilgrim, whose journey through life is often compared to a dark night, because we are surrounded by unbelief and immorality in the world, where many suffer from unjust laws and political systems. Others suffer from oppression because of their faith in Jesus. The world about us is weighed down by the burden of its own rebellion against God, and there seems no relief, for she will not seek God. She seeks, instead, to destroy the Church which houses God's presence and the solution to her problems. The only solution for the pilgrim lies in prayer to God.

Like the pilgrims of old, we must learn to fix our eyes on the Lord until He shows us His mercy in our world situation. The believers must stand in the breach for all those who do not understand, and for all those who do not believe, until God's solution to our situation is revealed (see Psalm 106:23). Spiritual pilgrims do not walk alone, just for their own benefit. They are the remnant through whom the many will be saved, even without their knowledge; another sign of God's incredible love. The cost is high, for they must live in total surrender to God in everything, even in the most trivial things. But they know that true freedom lies in this absolute surrender to the will of God and His sovereign Lordship over our lives. It makes them the happiest people on earth, and this is no small compensation for the price of surrender!

The surrendered person has found paradise on earth, and lives, even now, in the joy and peace of an unbroken relationship of love with God. He experiences true personal freedom, for he has learned, like Peter, to keep his eyes on the Lord, not on the wind and the waves of the stormy sea of life around him, so he magnifies the Lord, not the problem. Because of this stance, he experiences miracles in his life, because the obstacles to God's loving intervention are removed. Christians should not so much believe in the impossible, but do it!

Nevertheless, Christians must accept the contempt of the unbeliever as part of their lot, for the unbeliever does not share their vision and considers them foolish, and so rejects them. The world of the rich laughs them to scorn too, for their god is money and the worldly power that it buys, and the pilgrim is very often bereft of both. Jesus, the greatest pilgrim, and the leader of those on the way, had to take the contempt of the world before us, especially during His Passion, when the world poured its scorn onto Him for being foolish enough to think that He could change it and transform it by love alone. He has won for us the grace and the power to continue that transforming work in a world that will never appreciate what is being done for it, because it is blind to the presence of God in its midst, and deaf to His Word, so that its people cannot see, hear or understand, else they would be converted and live (see Matthew 13:15).

28

Psalm 126:
"It was like a Dream!"

This song of deliverance, which captures the delirious joy and profound relief of the Israelites returning home from captivity, found equal expression among the early Christians celebrating the joy of Easter, with its message of deliverance from all spiritual bondage. For the individual pray-er too there are times when only Psalm 126 can capture the mood.

When the Lord delivered Sion from bondage,
It seemed like a dream.
Then was our mouth filled with laughter,
on our lips there were songs.

The heathens themselves said: "What marvels
the Lord worked for them!"
What marvels the Lord worked for us!
Indeed we were glad.

Deliver us, O Lord, from our bondage
as streams in dry land.
Those who are sowing in tears
will sing when they reap.

They go out, they go out, full of tears,
carrying seed for the sowing:
they come back, they come back, full of song,
carrying their sheaves

(vv. 1–6).

The worshipping community, gathered in the presence of God, look away from their present need (see vv. 4–6), to review their past experience of God, and learn from it what to do now. They remember their ecstatic joy when they were released from bondage after seventy years; the happiness of returning to their own land, and their own Temple, even though it meant that they had to rebuild it. They attribute their deliverance to the miraculous intervention of God on their behalf, an act that made even the pagan nations, among whom they lived, give praise to God. There was no proud boasting about her election by God then, just gratitude and joy, so that the pagan nations rejoiced with her in her second exodus to Israel. Entering once again into these events in memory, the community can rejoice in God for His great mercy in the past, and let this give her hope for a like deliverance now, in her present trouble (vv. 1–3).

Reassured by the memory of God's loving-kindness in the past, the people turn to God and humbly request a miracle in the present. To turn the dry parched land of the Negeb in the South into streams of water was the miracle requested with such childlike simplicity. Since God is the God of the impossible, and He had already demonstrated this in the deliverance of the captives, the community could pray with real authority and hope in God for the new deliverance.

To express their prayer the psalmist uses the image of sowing and reaping. In the ancient world, the time of sowing seed was considered to be a time of mourning, while the reaping of the harvest was the time for rejoicing. It was the dying and rising theme as seen in nature. Through it the people expressed their faith in the life-giving power of God, who transforms our present sufferings by showing us the way through them to future hope – God's way of leading us from darkness to light (see Isaiah 44:3).

The early Church understood the delirious joy of this lovely psalm when the shock of the Resurrection of Jesus first dawned on her on Easter Day. "He is risen!", resounded everywhere, yet none could comprehend this greatest of all of God's interventions in the history of man. It was really true that Jesus had delivered His people from every spiritual bondage, and as this is the root of all other types of bondage, it was the beginning of "Paradise regained". The new life of adoption as God's children was now open to all nations, for God wanted all men to be saved and come to the knowledge of the truth (see Acts 10:34–35). Jesus had kept His promise to come back to His own (see John 14:18), and He brought them joy and peace that would last for ever (see John 14:27, 16:16, 20:19–23). He also fulfilled the great Messianic promise to give the outpouring of the Spirit to the Church and to the world (see John 7:37, 20:23). They were now filled with the Holy Spirit and the power of God, full of joy and peace, and a radiance that was Heaven-born.

Nevertheless, they were not allowed to stand about celebrating for ever, as there was a world out there to be saved. Jesus commissioned them to go out into this unwelcoming arena of hardened unbelief, to sow the seed of God's Word up and down the furrows of every land. Their mission would entail persecution, deprivation of every kind, and martyrdom in the end; hence the seed would be sown in tears, but the Church would rejoice to bring in a rich harvest of souls for God, as nation after nation was freed from its spiritual and material bondage – a miracle as great as the rivers in the Negeb. The dry spiritual desert of the world was to be transformed into fields ripe for harvesting, where sower and reaper would rejoice together. Jesus had sown the seed of the Word during His ministry and drenched it with the tears of His Passion and death; the Apostles were to reap this harvest, and then go on to sow with their own lives and martyrdom, which the next generation of Christians would reap, and so it would continue until the end of time (see John 4:34–38).

Those who really allow Jesus into their lives in such a way

that He is given the freedom to release them from all bondage know the joy of this psalm, for it is their song of deliverance too. The released drug addict, the depressive, the alcoholic, those released from despondency and despair, all know this wondrous joy, and can say: "Indeed we were glad!" Nevertheless this initial release, that starts these sufferers on the spiritual journey, even though it is a wonderful intervention of God, is only the beginning of the miracles. They do not yet know that the field of their souls is as dry and parched as ever the Negeb was, and only God can make the streams of living water flow there to produce growth (see Isaiah 58:11). Jesus must be allowed to pour out His Spirit on them in overflowing abundance if real growth is to take place (see John 4:10, 7:37). Besides, they must co-operate with the work of sanctification by working at repentance and doing God's will, while giving enough time to the study of God's Word, feeding on the Eucharist, and spending sufficient time in prayer.

There is a proportion between sowing and reaping, for thin sowing means thin reaping, and the more you sow the more you will reap (see 2 Corinthians 9:6). The person who is lazy in the things of the spirit cannot expect a great harvest. Another factor is that we reap what we sow; if we sow in the field of self-indulgence, then we reap a harvest of corruption; but if we sow in the field of the Spirit we shall reap a harvest of eternal life. The choice is ours (see Galatians 6:7–8). We also need to learn patience in waiting for the harvest too! Spiritual harvests come very slowly, and many people miss them because they do not persevere, but when they do come, they are permanent.

The greatest deliverance a person can know this side of death is the deliverance from the clinging self. He will be freed to experience the full joy of being God's child, and his journey ahead is into permanent joy and peace. Those who know this reality in their personal experience can enter fully into Psalm 126. This deliverance is like a dream; we can hardly believe it has happened to us. Then is our mouth full of laughter and song, and we sing that "He who is Mighty has done great things" for us. This liberated person will go on to do great work in releasing other captives, and so the story goes on. . . .

29

Psalm 127:
Unless the Lord Build

This short poem, which is attributed to King Solomon, takes up three of our most common and universal preoccupations, namely, building, security, and the raising of the family. It asks the important question: What does it all amount to? Where is it all going? Will there be any permanence to our activities? Will we leave any footprints in the sands of time?

If Solomon did indeed write this psalm, it is a great pity that he did not appropriate its lessons to his own great building projects, to the security of his own state, and to the proper running of his own enormous household. His kingdom was in ruin, divided for ever, at the end of his reign (see 1 Kings 11:11ff), and he allowed his foreign wives to turn him away from the true worship of the living God (see 1 Kings 11:1ff).

This psalm proclaims that man's schemes come to nothing, whereas that which comes from the hand of God is both strong and permanent.

If the Lord does not build the house,
in vain do its builders labour;
if the Lord does not watch over the city,
in vain does the watchman keep vigil.

In vain is your earlier rising,
your going later to rest,
you who toil for the bread you eat:
when he pours gifts on his beloved while they slumber.

Truly sons are a gift from the Lord,
a blessing, the fruit of the womb.
Indeed the sons of youth
are like arrows in the hand of a warrior.

O the happiness of the man
who has filled his quiver with these arrows!
He will have no cause for shame
when he disputes with his foes in the gateways
(vv. 1–5).

In a nutshell, verses 1–2 proclaim that all human endeavour which leaves God out of account is in vain, is worthless and leads nowhere. Three times the verdict "in vain" is given on all God-less activities. This is a radical denunciation of the attitude to work which claims that man can run and service his home, society and country disregarding God's will and God's laws for that home, society and land. God is Lord of history and very much involved with His creatures. He has definite plans for each individual, and each nation, which we neglect at our peril.

History is that complex interaction between God's plans for mankind, and our free co-operation with them, or our decision to act independently of them. When we rely on our own power and ingenuity we show our mistrust of God, and our lack of confidence in God's loving designs for us. Consequently we carry the burdens of family, society and nation unaided by God because we will not accept any help. We become enslaved by the treadmill of work, of social and political problems where we must take decisions as if we were God. The state then decides who will live and who will die, who will be helped and who will be abandoned to starve to death in poverty, loneliness and despair. What a burden to take on when it is all in vain, when God's Law would ensure the rights of the individual, make the family secure, and bring stability and peace to the nation.

It is not God's plan that we should eat the bread of

anxiety and endless toil (see Matthew 6:25–34), over-burdened with problems. He wants to teach us a more excellent way, not the way of sloth and inactivity, but that of surrender to His wise and perfect plan for each person, each nation and for the world. Reliance on God is the way of peace, where we carry out His will, with His help, and allow Him to be God for us. "Set your hearts on his kingdom first, and on his righteousness, and all these other things will be given you as well" (Matthew 6:33; J.B.). No wonder, then, that the psalmist says that all our endless labour without God is in vain, when He is prepared to see to all our needs if we submit to His ways. God pleads with us to give Him the burdens (see Matthew 11:28–30) and just accept from Him the light "yoke" of loving service to Him and to our neighbour, which will ensure that everyone is cared for according to their real needs. The perfect combination comes when God is allowed to *be* God, and we co-operate with His loving designs. This gives us an inner freedom from the anxieties of the world, which enables us to achieve lasting happiness while we are used effectively by God to rebuild the Church and society.

Perhaps the incident where the gospel shows us Jesus asleep in the boat, with a storm raging round Him, is a good pictorial representation of the teaching in this psalm (see Luke 8:22–25). The Son of God did not sleep from a slothful refusal to work, but as necessary rest following His labours in building up the Kingdom of God. He slept, confident that His father, the keeper of Israel, who neither slumbers nor sleeps, was in perfect control of every eventuality (see Psalm 121:4). He was resting in God. The frantic activity and strain of self-effort on the part of the disciples did nothing to improve conditions in the boat. The relaxed sleep of Jesus manifested a greater confidence in God than all the anxiety and fear of the others. Jesus, therefore, was the One through whom God could work to deal with the situation and calm the storm. Relaxed confidence in God brought the victory where frenetic activity only brought failure, pain and frustration – a good lesson for those who run our families, and our countries, if only they were willing to learn.

The family is the basic unit of both society and Church. In the Old Testament, to have a family was regarded as a blessing; not to have one, a curse. The gift of children was seen as evidence of divine favour (see Genesis 30:2, 22–24, etc). A family raised in the image of God was real wealth, not only for the parents, but also for the nation. God alone is the builder and architect of the family. Parents are His collaborators, who must co-operate with His plans for each child, and for the family as a whole, for He alone knows what the end product should be. Both the Church and the nation are as strong and as healthy as the family. When family life breaks down the Church and society begin to fall apart too, for the family is the basic unit of both. The result is anarchy.

If God is barred from the home, the builders of both society and nation labour in vain, because it is in the home that young people learn the principles of living in society, and become responsible citizens. It is there that they learn how to live a life that is worthwhile, fruitful and according to the mind of God. The home is where one learns the selfless loving service and self-sacrifice that is needed in later life to help build both Church and nation. For this enormous task, the parents, who can really be called the builders of the nation, must bring the presence of God into the home, and initiate that communication with God that will enable their children to grow to full spiritual maturity. Unless the parents build with the Lord, and in submission to Him, they will labour in vain, and live to see their failure in the irresponsible or criminal activity of their children.

The final message from this psalm is: build with the Lord if you want to secure the future of your nation, and if you want the world to continue as our home; otherwise some foolish world leader, in his pretence at playing God, may decide that you or your nation or your world should no longer exist.

30

Psalm 131:
Serene Joy

This tiny psalm is a literary gem with a brilliance all its own among the many jewels of the Psalter. It is a song of mature yet wonderfully tender, childlike faith and trust in God. Attributed to David, it reflects the quiet maturity of a person who has found fulfilment in God.

> O Lord, my heart is not proud
> nor haughty my eyes.
> I have not gone after things too great
> nor marvels beyond me.
>
> Truly I have set my soul
> in silence and peace.
> A weaned child on its mother's breast,
> even so is my soul.
>
> O Israel, hope in the Lord
> both now and for ever
> (vv. 1–3).

David comes before God in prayer, utterly open and unafraid to let God see what really is the condition of his heart. The pride and ambition of his youth are gone now, as is any presumption or leaning on his own strength. They are cast aside for the worthless things they are (see Philippians 3:7–9). He is no longer playing "god" to himself or others. He has learned, instead, to let God be God, and has accepted the lowliness of his own position. He recognizes the limitations of his own creature-hood, and so does not claim to know or understand everything. He will not try to raise himself up to some false level of importance. He has found peace in accepting the truth about himself, and so he can relax in the presence of God, much like a child in its mother's arms which has stopped its useless fretting and grabbing at its mother's breast, because it has learned to trust the mother's love, and also because it has discovered that there was a person behind the comfort it felt in being there. When the child begins to recognize the mother and trust her love, then it can relax. It is the same in our relationship with God; we can stop our anxious fretting and worrying once we realize that God is not just the supplier of all our needs, but more importantly, that He is a father who loves us and cares for us with infinite love.

When David declares that he has "set" his soul in silence and peace, he is saying that he has struggled, probably for many years, to calm the ceaseless surging of pride, arrogance and worldly ambition that strive for dominance in our lives. This fight against nature's struggle for honour, wealth and importance, meant that he had laboured to enter into his rest (see the Letter to the Hebrews 3:7–4:11). This peace and calm is not the inactivity of the foolish virgin who does nothing to prepare for the meeting with the Lord. It is, rather, the action of the wise virgin who co-operates on a daily basis with the grace that is available in ordinary things (see Matthew 25:1–13). We do not come to peace of heart without waging war on sin in ourselves, so it is the calm after the storm that is celebrated in this psalm. Besides, the peace and contentment which follow are such that one forgets the awful struggles that preceded them, and the many humiliating failures that have strewn one's path to the place of rest in God. All anxiety and fear vanish in the marvellous experience of union with God, and the heart is now captivated by the mutual love that quenches all thirst (see John 4:7). God is desired for Himself alone, not just for His gifts and graces. It is with this mature love and confident trust that he begs the whole nation to give fully to

God, so that the nation, too, may enter into the rest promised by God, which she rarely, if ever, experiences (see Exodus 33:14, Deuteronomy 12:10, etc).

Humility of heart is the necessary disposition if one is to come to complete rest from all striving and to permanent peace. Out of all the great qualities of His soul Jesus asked us to imitate only a few: ". . . learn from me, for I am gentle and humble in heart, and you will find rest for your souls" (see Matthew 11:29). When He acted as a slave, washing the feet of His faithful eleven at the Last Supper, Jesus said: "I have given you an example so that you may copy what I have done for you" . . . "Now that you know this, happiness will be yours if you behave accordingly" (see John 13:15,17; J.B.). The disciples found it difficult to grasp that it was not possible to humiliate the Son of God, because His greatness only shone with greater brilliance in His humility. An emperor is still the emperor even if he serves at table, but the humble service reveals a quality in him that is truly attractive, and does not at all detract from his dignity.

Presenting a little child to His disciples, Jesus told them about the revolution in their thinking that would be necessary for them to acquire humility of heart (see Matthew 18:1–4). If anyone wanted to be first, which represents the worldly position of pride and ambition, then Jesus asked them to take the opposite place, namely, to make himself last of all, and servant of all (Mark 9:35). This demands the death of the clinging self which keeps us in bondage to all kinds of fears and anxieties, and a battle must be fought and won before God is put in control of the life. It is necessary, therefore, to be weaned from all worldly ambition if we are to be free to relate to God in quiet confidence, peace and childlike trust.

St Paul showed how he mastered this struggle in a brilliant exposition of humility in Philippians chapter 2. The humble of heart are self-effacing, thinking of others all the time. They are in competition with no one; they are fully occupied with the imitation of Jesus' self-giving in the incarnation, life, Passion, death and Resurrection. He who has put all worldly ambition aside (Philippians 3) is now content with God's daily providential care for all His creatures (Philippians 4:11f), and he can be happy and content in his union with Christ (Philippians 4:4–9).

31

Psalm 139:
The Hound of Heaven

In Psalm 139, which is attributed to David, we reach one of the highest pinnacles of contemplation in the Psalter. Nowhere are the great attributes of God – His omnipresence, His omniscience and His omnipotence – set forth so strikingly as in this psalm. It stands pre-eminent, both for its lofty thought and wonderfully expressive language; language which reveals the depth and tenderness of the relationship of man and God, where man is not crushed by his all-knowing, all-filling and all-powerful God. This psalm is thought to have been the inspiration for Francis Thompson's lovely poem *The Hound of Heaven*, and I have used this title as a reminder.

O Lord, you search me and you know me,
you know my resting and my rising,
you discern my purpose from afar.
You mark when I walk or lie down,
all my ways lie open to you.

Before ever a word is on my tongue
you know it, O Lord, through and through.
Behind and before you besiege me,
your hand ever laid upon me.
Too wonderful for me, this knowledge,
too high, beyond my reach

(vv. 1–6).

Verses 1–6 deal with the all-seeing God, and express His omniscience in the lucid style of one lost in adoration, rather than in a dry doctrinal statement that would leave us unmoved. Here we are invited to join the psalmist in his wonder and awe that he is so encompassed by God. He addresses God in amazement that he is fully known in his innermost being, his waking and sleeping habits are known to God, and have been sifted and discerned for truth. God is completely familiar with all his ways, and to such an extent that before thoughts are formulated in his mind they are known to Him. God's hand is upon his whole life, and the knowledge of this is almost frightening. We can immediately see that hypocrisy before God is superlative folly! (see Matthew 9:4, John 1:47, Hebrews 4:13).

The realization that we are so completely known by God can be perceived by us as both good news and bad news together. For many who are entering into relationship with the Lord in a personal way for the first time, it can make it easier for healing grace to work in them. Since God already knows all the facts, confessing them before Him is easier, especially when it is pointed out that God loves the person in his present condition anyway. This can be very consoling to one who has not previously experienced love, for to love and be loved involves knowing and being known thoroughly. The realization of being known so fully and yet loved so uniquely by God is wonderful good news indeed.

For anyone who wishes to hide from God or keep their distance, this knowledge could be interpreted as "Big Brother is watching you!" This person feels that God is spying on his freedom, and spoiling his fun. Some could be terrorized, others could even come to hate God. For all of us who contemplate God's reality, and have not reached the pinnacle of perfection, there must be a holy fear, which spurs us on to greater efforts to build up the relationship of love with God, because only perfect love will cast out all fear (see 1 John 4:18).

O where can I go from your spirit,
or where can I flee from your face?
If I climb the heavens, you are there.
If I lie in the grave, you are there.

If I take the wings of the dawn
and dwell at the sea's furthest end,
even there your hand would lead me,
your right hand would hold me fast.

If I say: "Let the darkness hide me
and the light around me be night,"
even darkness is not dark for you
and the night is as clear as the day
(vv. 7–12).

It is not surprising that the instinct of the psalmist is to run from this all-knowing God, but where can he run to? No one has to tell us that we are not pure enough for God's presence, and so the urge to flee from the face of God is as old as the fall itself. The poet realizes, though, that it is as useless to flee from God as it is for a small child to run away from its parents, who are the source of its life, security and hope, and without whose tender love it cannot survive.

Taking the sweep of the universe into his vision, the psalmist surveys all of creation to demonstrate that God is everywhere, and that the very possibility of finding oneself somewhere where God is not is ludicrous. Being a pure spirit, there is no place outside the sphere of His power. Neither for the good nor the wicked is there any escape from the omnipresence of God. Whether one goes up to the heights of Heaven or into the depths of *sheol* or death, God is there. The speed of the light that heralds the morning, and the distant horizon of the sea both proclaim His presence. Nor will the darkness of night afford any refuge. Man may not penetrate the darkness, but nothing is impenetrable to God. Man seeks in vain to find God's limits, yet the hand that pursues him is one that holds him in love.

When Jesus came to reveal that God was a father to us, and One who is motivated by infinite love, that His designs towards us were all mercy and grace, then the New Testament writers gave us the teaching of this psalm from the opposite angle, as we see in Romans 8:31–39: "With God on our side who can be against us? For I am certain of this: neither death nor life, no angel, no prince, nothing that exists, nothing still to come, nor any power, nor height nor depth, nor any created thing can ever come between us and the love of God made visible in Christ Jesus our Lord." This changes the element of fearfulness expressed by the psalmist into a triumphant declaration of security in God.

> For it was you who created my being,
> knit me together in my mother's womb.
> I thank you for the wonder of my being,
> for the wonders of all your creation.
>
> Already you knew my soul,
> my body held no secret from you
> when I was being fashioned in secret
> and moulded in the depths of the earth.
>
> Your eyes saw all my actions,
> they were all of them written in your book;
> every one of my days was decreed
> before one of them came into being.
>
> To me, how mysterious your thoughts,
> the sum of them not to be numbered!
> If I count them, they are more than the sand;
> to finish, I must be eternal, like you
>
> (vv. 13–18).

This third section of the psalm carries forward the ideas of the first two; God not only sees the invisible, and penetrates the inaccessible, but is intimately involved with us. He who transcends all time and space is involved in both, in the work of our own creation, and since we cannot escape from His presence we run into His arms, and find that this removes all fear in the intimacy of unconditional love.

Having penetrated the depths of both heaven and *sheol* we now descend into the dark mysteries of the womb, and find that there, too, the hand of God is at work in our pre-natal development. It is awesome indeed to ponder the fact that He who fixes the stars and plans their course through the heavens has also fixed my body together with such immense detail, and plans the course of my life through its earthly and heavenly journeys. Between God's enormous plans for the universe, and His extraordinary attention to detail in the making of a human being, we are left simply to praise and adore. The problem of fear that held us initially is answered in the realization of His knowledge of us. Now we know that it is *loving* knowledge, and that makes the difference. It is not the knowledge of a judge who wishes to condemn, but that of a father who wants to help and guide us to the fullness of life.

Mother earth, the mother of all living things, is also a dark womb that houses us throughout our earthly pilgrimage, as God's delicate hands work with us in the secret place of our spirit, to fashion us into the fully redeemed person, the ideal man or woman. During all his days, therefore, man needs to look to this wonderful knowledge of God to guide him. Yet he is aware that somehow God keeps a record of everything in "The Book of the Living" (see Exodus 32:32–33, Psalm 69:28), and this knowledge of being one of the elect gives the poet a sense of security. He is not only God's creature but also part of God's family.

So overwhelmed is the poet by the contemplation of all

these wonders that he now exclaims in reverential awe that the mystery of God is impenetrable, and all His thoughts inscrutable. To comprehend the living God one would need to *be* God! As for us creatures, it will take all eternity to try to grasp the wonder of His being, and this will keep us occupied with praise and adoration.

> O God, that you would slay the wicked!
> Men of blood, keep far away from me!
> With deceit they rebel against you
> and set your designs at naught.
>
> Do I not hate those who hate you,
> abhor those who rise against you?
> I hate them with a perfect hate
> and they are foes to me.
>
> O search me, God, and know my heart.
> O test me and know my thoughts.
> See that I follow not the wrong path
> and lead me in the path of life eternal
> (vv. 19–24).

The abrupt return to everyday realities from the heights of contemplation comes to us with a shock. Suddenly the psalmist is faced again with the problem of evil-doers, and his reaction to them must be interpreted in the light of the vision he has just seen. The rebellion of the wicked is intolerable to him now, and he rejects their evil influence vehemently. His reaction reminds one of Moses seeing the idolatry of Israel on his return from sojourning with God for forty days on Mount Sinai (see Exodus 32:15–24). The reverential awe of God is behind this, but his understanding of God is limited, for he has not realized that the presence of the just and the wicked on the earth is all part of God's inscrutable ways. He is also limited by the thinking of his own day, where justice had to be *seen* to be done.

A greater revelation was yet to come, through Jesus, of God's compassion for His wayward children, and His incomprehensible love that would make Jesus die for the release of sinners. The psalmist here thinks that only the innocent are acceptable to God, so he protests his innocence by declaring loudly that he hates evil with all his heart. He had to learn that while God, too, hates sin, yet He loves the sinner infinitely, and does not wish his death but only his salvation. At the same time the poet is right in his insight that commitment to God in holiness demands a rejection of all fellowship with sin (see 2 Corinthians 6:14–18).

The psalm finishes in a mood opposite to that of its beginning. Here the poet is much more confident in this God whom he has come to know so much better, and so he asks the all-knowing God to put a search-light into his heart and expose the thoughts that are hidden there, so that he can receive guidance to go forward in his spiritual journey. Here we see a very important principle: that knowledge which is theoretical will merely make us self-important, but knowledge gained through experience, especially when it is acted upon, will increase our maturity.

32

Psalm 145:
Praise God!

This beautiful hymn is the last of the psalms attributed to
David, and the introduction to the final chorus which
closes the Book of Praises, the Psalter. Although it is an
alphabetical psalm, the grandeur of the theme releases it
from bondage to its structure.

> I will give you glory, O God my King,
> I will bless your name for ever.
>
> I will bless you day after day
> and praise your name for ever.
> The Lord is great, highly to be praised,
> his greatness cannot be measured.
>
> Age to age shall proclaim your works,
> shall declare your mighty deeds,
> shall speak of your splendour and glory,
> tell the tale of your wonderful works.
>
> They will speak of your terrible deeds,
> recount your greatness and might.
> They will recall your abundant goodness;
> age to age shall ring out your justice
> (vv. 1–7).

David, himself a great king, addresses God as the
sovereign Lord of the universe. He lifts up his eyes above
petty mundane things, and above all personal interest, to
focus his attention on God alone. This is the first step in

real praise. The second is a clear decision to praise God regardless of personal circumstances. The psalms of praise abound with the statement "I will . . ." The third rule for praise is to have a motive: here God is praised for His grandeur, His greatness, His marvellous works, His splendour and His glory. True praise is also timeless, for it deals with the unsearchable sublimity and majesty of God, and each generation needs to join in the praise of the last generation in order to express its worship and thanks to God. The result is that the praise of mankind then flows down through human history like a swelling river making for the great eternal sea, where heaven and earth join in its praise of God.

David could not have known how literally his words would be fulfilled, for age after age have used his words to praise God! The wonders that God worked for his age pale into insignificance before the glory of the Christ event. Yet his words in this timeless psalm adequately praise God for both. In fact, his generation and ours join together in thanking God for all His redemptive works. There is room for the festal shouts of joy to ring out year after year to acclaim the miraculous mighty deeds of God on behalf of His children. Those who have entered personally into intimacy with God will spontaneously express the wonder of it all day after day in personal praise.

> The Lord is kind and full of compassion,
> slow to anger, abounding in love.

> How good is the Lord to all,
> compassionate to all his creatures

(vv. 8–9).

To have to deal with a remote God of great splendour and majesty may evoke terror and fear, but hardly love.

The greatest praise is reserved for God when He revealed His splendour and majesty through His lovingkindness and compassion to all His creatures, so that love and gratitude are the spontaneous response of His children to this good father. Verse 8 is almost word for word the self-revelation of God to Moses on Sinai (see Exodus 34:6), given in response to Moses' plea that God should tell the people what He was *really* like. The fact that God showed Himself tender-hearted, made Moses – and all of God's servants after him – ecstatic with joy, because it meant that God could be touched by our needs, and therefore would respond with more of His saving interventions on our behalf. Witness the reaction of Jesus on seeing the grief of Mary after the death of her brother Lazarus in John 11. He was so deeply touched that He wept, and went to the tomb to raise Lazarus from the dead. Jesus was tender-hearted, and this lovingkindness of God is universal, reaching not only all men but also all other creatures too (see Luke 12:24, 27, Jonah 4:1–11).

All your creatures shall thank you, O Lord,
and your friends shall repeat their blessing.
They shall speak of the glory of your reign
and declare your might, O God,

to make known to men your mighty deeds
and the glorious splendour of your reign.
Yours is an everlasting kingdom;
your rule lasts from age to age

(vv. 10–13).

David moves now from praising God for His wonderful redemptive acts to the rule of His Kingdom which embraces all mankind. All the empires of this world fade away before the universal reign of God which will last for ever, for it takes neither its power nor authority from this world (see John 18:36–37). Even the kings in the ancient world acknowledged this – we read verse 13 repeated on the lips of Nebuchadnezzar in Daniel 3:33. Human powers all come to an end but God's power is eternal. It is the psalmist's way of saying: *Sic transit gloria mundi* (1 Timothy 1:17).

The Lord is faithful in all his words
and loving in all his deeds.
The Lord supports all who fall
and raises all who are bowed down.

The eyes of all creatures look to you
and you give them their food in due time.
You open wide your hand,
grant the desires of all who live.

The Lord is just in all his ways
and loving in all his deeds.
He is close to all who call him,
who call on him from their hearts.

He grants the desires of those who fear him,
he hears their cry and he saves them.
The Lord protects all who love him;
but the wicked he will utterly destroy.

Let me speak the praise of the Lord,
let all mankind bless his holy name
for ever, for ages unending

(vv. 14–21).

This section completes and crowns this wonderful psalm by extolling the graciousness of God towards everyone. God's goodness, declared in verses 7–9, is now illustrated towards those in need. He keeps His promises by showing fatherly care towards those who have gone astray, and by offering comfort and relief to those who are overburdened from whatever source. God also supplies the spiritual and material hunger of all His creatures, and does so in joyous abundance – expressed in that wonderful phrase: "You open wide your hand (to) grant the desires of all who live." The feeding is, therefore, not confined to the material, but to all of life's needs, and there is a generosity in the giving that contrasts with the miserliness of human methods of help (see Matthew 6:25–34).

God's goodness extends far beyond the mere offering of help in time of need, marvellous though that is. God's nature is love, and so all His actions in our regard are motivated by love, by His desire to reach out to us and draw us close to Himself in loving union. This He does especially for those who open up to Him in prayer; they have the joy of answered prayer, where those who keep their distance from Him are unaware of this great privilege. The closer one comes to Him the more one discovers that *He is love* and can be touched by a loving response from us. His readiness to answer prayer is only amazing if one remembers His splendour and majesty emphasized earlier in the psalm.

Finally, we hear of God's protection for the "good" and His destruction of the "wicked". It would hardly be a psalm about real life if there were no mention of the wicked, and it would definitely not be a psalm of David! God's righteousness is upheld in the end, for His love is a just and holy love. Those who experience His protection are those who have entered into a life of loving obedience to His Word, while those who are "destroyed" are those who choose to live life without any protection from God, and so fall victim to their own sinfulness and to the wickedness they find in the world.

The psalm ends with David full of the praise of God himself, and in union with all of creation in its praise.

Uniting his personal testimony to that of "all flesh" he completes his song by stating the ultimate purpose that all creatures serve, namely, the praise of God. His vision, as wide as the universe, is as lasting as eternity.

33

Psalm 146:
Why Trust in God?

Five joyous psalms of praise, each of them beginning and ending with Halleluia, bring the Psalter to a close. They form the happy ending to the song book of the Lord, which made men search for truth and righteousness amid the darkness of this world, with its violence and evil, and helped them listen to the cries of distress, and the prayers for vindication from the innocent who suffered at the hands of the wicked. Likewise it made us search the darkness of our own souls, and admit the sinfulness that was there, so that we too would cry out for deliverance. It showed us the weary journey to new life and hope that we had to take if we really wanted inner freedom, and warned us that we would suffer both from the scorn of the unbelievers and the doubts that arise so strongly from inside of ourselves.

The journey is completed now and, full of joy and happiness, safe from the onslaughts of the enemy, we can rest confident in our union with the Lord, and join the choirs of angels and saints in heaven, as well as the voices of all creation, in the everlasting praise of God, which will be our happy work for all eternity, where we shall rest from our labours but not from our praise. These psalms remind us of the promise that God would wipe away the tears from every cheek, when there would be no more death or sorrow or pain, for all the former things would have passed away, and paradise would be regained. There would remain only a redeemed people full of joy, celebrating the goodness of God in their continual praise (see Isaiah 25:6–10).

There have been other psalms which showed the sunshine side of our relationship with God, where the people laughed, sang, danced and clapped their hands in joyful praise and thanksgiving, but we always had to return to the weariness of the everyday struggles. It is only in the grand finale to the Psalter that we have an almost cloudless sky, and utter stillness in the earth, when the storms of life are over. These five psalms form a pentad of praise, a fitting finish to the five-part work of the Psalter which, according to ancient authorities, is a commentary on the Pentateuch, the five-part work of the Torah (the Law). The Midrash (commentary) on Psalm 1:1 says: "Moses gave to the Israelites the five Books of the Law; and corresponding with these David gave them the five Books of the Psalter."

Alleluia!

My soul, give praise to the Lord;
I will praise the Lord all my days,
make music to my God while I live.

Put no trust in princes,
in mortal men in whom there is no help.
Take their breath, they return to clay
and their plans that day come to nothing.

He is happy who is helped by Jacob's God,
whose hope is in the Lord his God,
who alone made heaven and earth,
the seas and all they contain.

It is he who keeps faith for ever,
who is just to those who are oppressed.
It is he who gives bread to the hungry,
the Lord, who sets prisoners free,

the Lord who gives sight to the blind,
who raises up those who are bowed down,
the Lord, who protects the stranger
and upholds the widow and orphan.

It is the Lord who loves the just
but thwarts the path of the wicked.
The Lord will reign for ever,
Sion's God from age to age

Alleluia!

(vv. 1–10).

This psalm opens with a general call to praise God in the Halleluia, which means "Praise ye the Lord", but is quickly followed by the psalmist calling upon himself to enter fully into the general praise, and his intention is to do so all his life, not just on this one occasion. He has learned from the experiences of life not to put his trust in frail mortal man, no matter how important the person may be on the social scale. Once the breath of life is taken from the mighty even they return to the dust from which they came, and all their pomp and pageantry disappear like the morning mist. They are hardly buried before they are forgotten; this holds true for both paupers and potentates! God alone, our creator and redeemer, is everlasting. We can safely put our trust in Him, especially since He revealed His loving-kindness to us in redemption (vv. 1–6).

It is not without good reason that the negative warning about putting our trust in mortal man precedes the positive praise concerning our right trust in God. Only when man realizes the transitory nature of human supports will real trust in God become possible. As long as we have any other prospect of help we do not have unreserved confidence in God, but when all ephemeral support has been removed we are free to throw ourselves fully upon God's infinite goodness, and discover for ourselves how great He is.

It is interesting that God is referred to here as "Jacob's God", and not the God of Abraham. Jacob is closer to most of us than the heroic Abraham. He was a man of guileful, grasping disposition, who lived an ordinary life of commonplace experience; a man who needed a real conversion in his life before God could use him. Yet he wrestled with God in prayer and was changed to "Israel", the father of the Chosen People. The aspect of God that we feel most comfortable with is Our Lord, the One who is the covenant God, who entered into relationship with us disregarding our sinfulness, and who continuously finds a way out for us when we fall from grace. Our Lord also loves us so much that He is willing to work with us to transform our lives, as He did for our father, Jacob.

The rest of the psalm details some of the redemptive actions of our Lord and God, and justifies the earlier exhortation to trust in God. It provides an eloquent picture of how the Old Testament believer perceived the value of the divine loving-kindness on which he based his life. All the incidents prove the same point by showing that the efficacy of the divine help is seen most clearly in the very things where human help fails. All those whom society rejects will find their help, their hope and their healing in God – the oppressed, the hungry, the prisoners (with no judgement as to whether they are guilty or innocent), the blind, those who are bowed down, the stranger, the widow and the orphan. The princes of the earth may have no time for these poor suffering people yet the king of the universe gives them His full time and attention; yet another example of how different God's ways are from ours. Here the psalmist is saying that God's power is made perfect in weakness (see 2 Corinthians 12:9). It is only when we recognize our own weakness and powerlessness that we can open up to His working in us, which is inhibited by our self-sufficiency and independence. The poor person who trusts in God knows that he is completely safe, and need have no fear of the wicked, for God is on his side, and He is the ruler of the universe from everlasting to everlasting. The wicked pale into the insignificance which they really deserve, while the poor are given the confidence that they should really have (vv. 6–10).

The vision of God given in these verses not only applies to the Father, but equally to the Son, for Jesus claimed that "My Father goes on working, and so do I" (see John 5:17). The attributes of God illustrated here were demonstrated by Jesus in His life and healing ministry. The Father's compassion toward the under-privileged and the down-trodden, was shown in His giving sight to the blind, releasing captives, and supporting the widow and the orphan. When Jesus announced His ministry in Nazareth for the first time, His mission statement contained the same words. He said: "The spirit of the Lord has been given to me, for He has anointed me. He has sent me to bring good news to the poor, to proclaim liberty to captives, and to the blind new sight, to set the down-trodden free, to proclaim the Lord's year of favour" (see Isaiah 61:1–2; J.B.). The coming of the Son of God to earth in the incarnation was to release the power of God into all those situations that needed redemption.

Reading this psalm in its New Testament perspective we can say that God has remained faithful to His people beyond their greatest expectations (see Ephesians 3:21), for He continues, throughout every generation, to give justice to those who are denied it. He continues to feed the hungry, whether the hunger is spiritual or temporal (see Matthew 5:6). He releases the spiritual and temporal captives, and gives healing to both the spiritually and materially blind. He cares for the widows and orphans of every age, and takes care of His friends. He did this in its most spectacular way through Jesus, His

Son, but continues to do it through the mystical body of Christ throughout the world. The Church can be seen to be the true body of Christ when it continues His mission to the poor and the needy of this world.

Let us join the psalmist in his praise for all eternity, and for the same motives: that of glorifying and praising God for His goodness to us, His undeserving children.

34

Psalm 147:
From a Grateful People to a Great God

The Greek Septuagint and the Latin Vulgate both divide
this psalm into two parts, calling verses 1–11 Psalm 146, and
verses 12–20 Psalm 147, but we are following the Hebrew
Bible which treats it as one psalm with two parts. The first
part, comprising verses 1–6, praises God as the lord of
history for His redeemed people. Verses 7–11 praise Him
as the creator and provider in nature; while verses 12–20
praise Him for His creative and life-giving Word.

Alleluia!

Praise the Lord for he is good;
sing to our God for he is loving:
to him our praise is due.

The Lord builds up Jerusalem
and brings back Israel's exiles,
he heals the broken-hearted,
he binds up all their wounds.
He fixes the number of the stars;
he calls each one by its name.

Our Lord is great and almighty;
his wisdom can never be measured.
The Lord raises the lowly;
he humbles the wicked to the dust.
Sing to the Lord, giving thanks;
sing psalms to our God with the harp
(vv. 1–7).

The psalm begins by praising God for His goodness in bringing back Israel's exiles, and for healing their broken hearts by gathering them once again in His Temple in Jerusalem. Presumably we are dealing with the post-exilic era, and close to the return of the exiles and the rebuilding of the Temple. He whose power is limitless – who alone fixes the stars in their places, and governs their course in the heavens – is big enough to deal with the remaining problems of the restoration of His afflicted people, and to deal with the wickedness of evil men.

His widom is shown in His dealings with His children, first in the chastening of exile, and then in the return of a humbled people to their ancestral home, and cannot be comprehended. It is hard to grasp that the hand that chastened is also the hand that heals. The Lord loves His people so much that He will allow them to be chastened when that is the only way to true life, but as soon as they are ready for real surrender to His will, which contains all life for them, He is ready to heal the wounds that His love inflicted (see Hosea 6:1–3).

> He covers the heavens with clouds;
> he prepares the rain for the earth,
> making mountains sprout with grass
> and with plants to serve man's needs.
> He provides the beasts with their food
> and young ravens that call upon him.
>
> His delight is not in horses
> nor his pleasure in warrior's strength.
> The Lord delights in those who revere him,
> in those who hope in his love
>
> (vv. 8–11).

From this second part one would gather that this psalm was used for the autumn feast, perhaps for the Feast of Tabernacles which was held in October, at the end of the dry season, when Israel prayed for rain and prepared for the winter months ahead. Here the poet looks with joy at God's provision for His chosen people in the giving of rain for the coming harvest, but also in His generous provision for all His creatures, down to the young ravens who cry to Him for food. The immense range of God's operations are just as marvellous in their vastness as in their attention to detail. God is so great that He provides everything that the earth needs, yet He is so loving that He hears the least cry of one of His creatures.

Jesus went even further than this in Matthew 6:25–34 where the flowers of the field are clothed in greater splendour than Solomon, and in Luke 12:4–12, where the little sparrows are cared for by a Father who is so detailed in His provision that it can be expressed thus: "Why, every hair on your head has been counted"! The even more amazing reality is that this great Father of the world delights in those who love Him just as any "Daddy" would; Jesus instructed us to call Him *Abba*, Daddy. This acknowledges His life-giving role as well as His role as our provider; the motive in each case is infinite love. Such a Father is to be trusted and praised with adoration.

O praise the Lord, Jerusalem!
Sion, praise your God!

He has strengthened the bars of your gates,
he has blessed the children within you.
He established peace on your borders,
he feeds you with the finest wheat.

He sends out his word to the earth
and swiftly runs his command.
He showers down snow white as wool,
he scatters hoar-frost like ashes.

He hurls down hailstones like crumbs.
The waters are frozen at his touch;
he sends forth his word and it melts them:
at the breath of his mouth the waters flow.

He makes his word known to Jacob,
to Israel his laws and decrees.
He has not dealt thus with other nations;
he has not taught them his decrees.

Alleluia!

(vv. 12–20).

This final section of the psalm weaves together the life-giving power and nourishment of God's Word, and of water. Water is the life force that enables growth to take place, it must be supplied by the Good God at the proper time and for the right seasons of the year. Without it drought and famine would ensue, with death by starvation for everyone in its wake. It is God's creative Word that supplies this life-giving water for us, and it is not only a heavenly gift; it also originates in the heavens. It comes down to us by the command of the Lord. Its power is to soften the earth and prepare it for life, but it nourishes that life too, for the growing thing will not develop without water, which forms part of its substance. This water comes in varied forms – rain, snow, hailstones, ice, and hoar-frost that bejewels the morning.

Water, in its functions, resembles the Word of God itself, which comes down from God to us, softening our hearts to prepare us for spiritual growth. Isaiah expressed these thoughts fully in chapter 55:11: "As the rain and the snow come down from the heavens and do not return without watering the earth, making it yield and giving growth to provide seed for the sower and bread for the eating, so the word that goes forth from my mouth does not return to me empty, without carrying out my will and succeeding in what it was sent to do" (J.B.). This life-giving Word of God was entrusted to Israel, but it was meant to fertilize the whole earth.

The same cycle is seen again, but in its fullness, when Jesus, who is the Word of God incarnate, came down from Heaven to dwell among us. He is both the living water who nourishes our life, and which must become part of us if we are to become the Children of God, but He is also the full expression of God and manifests to us God's will in its fullness. He came down from God and did not return to Him empty. Instead He accomplished everything the Father wanted for the redemption of the world (see John 1:1–14, 4:10–14, 14:6). Jesus not only came down from Heaven, but showed us the pathway back to the bosom of the father where we will praise Him for ever in eternal glory.

35

Psalm 148:
A Universal Symphony

This psalm, whose author is unknown, constitutes a Halleluia Chorus of such beauty and poetry that it defies analysis, even though it has a definite plan, which we shall see. It should be appreciated as a whole, listened to and, above all, experienced. It should be contemplated, or better still, sung, in the blazing glory of an evening sunset when the heart is opened to feel the presence and glory of God in the wonder of His creation. The psalm was used in the Temple liturgy in the post-exilic period, either by a choir or a soloist. It is a universal call to praise the Lord, which has two parts, as follows:

(1) Praise from the heavens (1–6)
   The call to praise (1–4)
   The motive for praise (5–6)

(2) Praise from the earth (7–14)
   The call to praise (7–12)
   The motive for praise (13–14)

Alleluia!

Praise the Lord from the heavens,
praise him from the heights.
Praise him, all his angels,
praise him, all his hosts.

Praise him, sun and moon,
praise him, shining stars.
Praise him, highest heavens
and the waters above the heavens.

Let them praise the name of the Lord.
He commanded: they were made.
He fixed them for ever,
gave a law which shall not pass away
(vv. 1–6).

This hymn of praise follows the course of God's revelation of Himself to man, seen first of all in His creation, then through the ministry of angels who are sent to help Him on His journey of salvation, until finally He reveals Himself. The pagan world worshipped the sun, moon and stars, and even God's own people were tempted to worship angels (see Colossians 2:18, Revelation 22:8f), but here they are all united in one call to prostrate themselves before the Living God and worship Him. There is no fear of misunderstanding for the writer names the heavens, the heights, the sun, moon and stars, with the mysterious rain above the heavens; they must praise God who is their maker and controller. He also calls upon the angelic hosts by name for they too must worship God (see Revelation 5:11–14).

Praise the Lord from the earth,
sea creatures and all oceans,
fire and hail, snow and mist,
stormy winds that obey his word;

all mountains and hills,
all fruit trees and cedars,
beasts, wild and tame,
reptiles and birds on the wing;

all earth's kings and peoples,
earth's princes and rulers;
young men and maidens,
old men together with children.

Let them praise the name of the Lord
for he alone is exalted.
The splendour of his name
reaches beyond heaven and earth.

He exalts the strength of his people.
He is the praise of all his saints,
of the sons of Israel,
of the people to whom he comes close.

Alleluia!

(vv. 7–14).

The first stanza began at the top, with the celestial heights, and worked down from there, but the second one begins in the depths and works up! The first begins with rational angelic beings, and the second ends with rational human beings. The celestial beings were to praise God for what He did in creation, as well as who He is, and what He does in maintaining and controlling that creation. Now the call to praise rings out to the depths of the earth, firstly from the oceans with their teeming life: then the elements are called upon, those same elements which God used to herald His approach on Sinai and elsewhere – fire, hail, stormy wind – which are known to obey His Word (see 1 Kings 19:11–13, Exodus 19:16–25).

Following this the plant and animal kingdoms are called to recognize their creator and sustainer; and lastly man himself, with all his kings and rulers, and with the whole community of Israel, comprising all ages and ranks; the author here is following the order of creation as given in Genesis. Man was the last to appear on the scene and so is

211

the last to be summoned in praise. This leaves him without excuse, for all creation is already praising God, and man has more reason for praise than all the rest of creation put together, because God, in His mercy, also chose a special people for Himself, bound to Him by covenant love, a people who were close to Him and cared for by Him. To them He had revealed both His name and His nature, His majesty and His love. They above all others are duty bound to praise Him.

St Bernard of Clairvaux, in his lament over the death of his brother Gerard, said: "Who could ever have loved me as he did? He was a brother by blood, but far more in the faith. God grant, Gerard, that I may not have lost thee, but that thou hast only gone before me; for, of a surety, thou hast joined those whom, in thy last night below, thou didst invite to praise God, when suddenly, to the surprise of all, thou, with a serene countenance and cheerful voice, didst commence chanting that Psalm, 'Praise ye the Lord from the heavens; praise Him in the heights. Praise ye Him, all his angels; praise ye Him all His hosts.' At that moment, O my brother, the day dawned on thee, though it was night to us; the night to thee was all brightness" (see Bernard's Sermons on the Canticle of Canticles).

36

Psalm 149:
Victory Celebration

This is the fourth of the Halleluia psalms which complete the Psalter. It is similar in form to the others, except for the presence of enemies, and the talk of judgement. There may be a verbal connection with Psalm 148:14; this ended with the call to Israel to praise God as the chosen people, but only after the whole of creation had been harnessed to the same wonderful work. The present psalm concentrates on the praises of Israel, and on the wonder that God's presence becomes more manifest when His people praise Him, and His power to rule and execute judgement on the godless is released into the world in a special way also.

Taken together these two psalms praise God as creator and redeemer, for here we join Israel in celebrating another victory over her many enemies. This psalm declares abundance of joy for God's people when they are really united with Him and, by the same token, abundance of terror to their enemies.

Alleluia!

Sing a new song to the Lord,
his praise in the assembly of the faithful.
Let Israel rejoice in its Maker,
let Sion's sons exult in their king.
Let them praise his name with dancing
and make music with timbrel and harp.

For the Lord takes delight in his people.
He crowns the poor with salvation.
Let the faithful rejoice in their glory,
shout for joy and take their rest.
Let the praise of God be on their lips
and a two-edged sword in their hand,

to deal out vengeance to the nations
and punishment on all the peoples;
to bind their kings in chains
and their nobles in fetters of iron;
to carry out the sentence pre-ordained;
this honour is for all his faithful.

Alleluia!
                                            (vv. 1–9).

The previous psalm called upon all creation to praise God, but here the call goes out to God's own people alone. This is a church celebration, where the new situation calls for a new song of praise, given to God with the time-honoured accompaniment of dancing, singing and the playing of musical instruments. It is public praise that is called for, not only in the sense that the whole congregation is involved, but, as we shall see in verse 7, the whole world is affected in its scope and power. Praise such as this presumes a living relationship with God, one where real conversion has taken place. The "old man" in us sees no reason to praise God for anything (see Ephesians 4:22), but the man who has experienced the saving grace of God will sing praise, and not only in public.

The note of joy dominates this final group of psalms, and prepares the way for the revelation of true joy in the New Testament, where it is one of the fruits of the spirit (see Galatians 5:22), and with peace is one of the characteristic signs of the presence of the Kingdom of God in the individual (see Romans 14:17). Joy and peace may describe the normal Christian life, but unfortunately not the normal life of many Christians.

The joy is not one-sided, for the Lord delights in His people too, most especially when they open their hearts to His redeeming grace. He is like a father delighting in the happiness and fulfilment of His children, after He has poured out the necessities of life upon them, realizing that their destiny depends entirely on His love. This two-way joy describes the deep sense of fulfilment and rest for the heart brought about by the life-giving and grace-filled relationship with God our father which is so well expressed by praise (vv. 1–5).

Joy and peace, praise and rest, do not express the total experience of relationship with God. The shadow side is the spiritual warfare which we would rather not have; we often ask that this chalice be removed from us, even though there is no spiritual victory without the battle which must precede it. For Israel, "holy war" was synonymous with her relationship with God. Here, as elsewhere in the Bible, we see that God taught her through her historical experience the principles that we, in the New Testament, need to learn for our spiritual walk with God. Like it or not, praise and spiritual warfare go hand in hand. The song and the sword work together, because the Kingdom of God can only be established with the defeat of the kingdom of darkness.

For Israel the song and the sword were understood literally, because she was used by God to punish the Canaanites on her first entry into the Promised Land: her orders were to wipe them out, and she did (see Genesis 15:13–16, Numbers 33:52). For us who live in the fullness of time, in the full brilliance of revelation, it is different, even though history demonstrates that many a Christian army marched forth literally to destroy other peoples, taking this psalm as their justification. If they did, they had not read in 2 Corinthians 10:4 that the weapons of our warfare are not carnal, yet they are powerful enough to bring down the

strongholds of human philosophy and arguments of unbelief that fight against the true knowledge of God. The
two-edged sword we hold in our hands is the Word of
God, which is the bulwark against all untruth (see the
Letter to the Hebrews 4:12).

For us, the battle is spiritual, but our need to be
militant for God is just as real and urgent. Paul told his
disciple Timothy to "fight the good fight of the faith",
and to hold out against all the opposition that the early
Church was experiencing from the pagan philosophers of
the day (see 1 Timothy 6:12). He instructed his converts
to arm themselves for the battle, using the image of a
Roman soldier, except that the "whole armour" was
spiritual (see Ephesians 6:12–18). The warfare we wage
is double; internal, against evil within ourselves, where
"every thought must be captured and put under
obedience to Christ" (see 2 Corinthians 10:5), and external, where we oppose the destructive powers of evil
which are bent on destroying the individual, society and
the world.

The punishment of the nations who are at enmity with
the Kingdom of God is left to the Lord Jesus Himself, in
the Book of Revelation, which describes the end of
human history. As the true Word of God incarnate, all
judgement was given to Him by the Father (see John
5:22), and He will come with His angelic hosts to execute
judgement on the whole world according to the infinite
just goodness of God. It will be done in such a way that
all nations will bend the knee and confess that Jesus is
Lord, to the great glory of God, who is creator, redeemer, father, friend, lover or judge, as we choose to
relate to Him, both individually and nationally.

The true victory of the individual is described in Revelation in the following wonderful words: "Now have the
salvation and power come, the reign of our God and the
authority of his Anointed One. For the accuser of our
brothers is cast out, who night and day accused them

before our God. They defeated him by the blood of the Lamb and the word of their testimony; love for life did not deter them from death. So rejoice, you heavens, and you that dwell therein" (Revelation 12:10–12a).

37

Psalm 150:
The Great Halleluia

At last we reach the final crashing crescendo of the Psalter, and it is all praise. The Psalter began with "Happy is the man", but ends with "Give Praise to the Lord!" It began with the two ways open to everyone, and demonstrated that people take different paths, some good, some evil. It ends with all evil eliminated – the chaff is gone: we are left with the true People of God expressing the highest sentiments of religion, for praise is the consummation of all religion. No division exists between earth or heaven, or within the community of God's people; none exists within any part of creation, for "all that breathes" joins in the praise of God with one mind and heart. This psalm, therefore, illustrates the final state of the Church, after everything has been renewed in Christ, when we stand together to celebrate for ever the praise of the Triune God for the marvel that He is and the wonders that He has done.

Between these two poles we have experienced with the psalm writers the normal ups and downs of the spiritual life. We went from the unbelief and rebellion of the nations in Psalm 2 to the consequences of the two ways in Psalm 3, where the good suffer at the hands of the wicked. We searched for peace of mind in Psalm 4, while contemplating the marvel of our election by God in Psalm 8, notwithstanding our nothingness. Psalm 19 showed us how to find God, either through nature or the Scriptures. Psalms 20 and 21 made us look for deeper depths than we might first suspect, for the psalms have a prophetic role in preparing us for the revelation of Messiah. Psalm 22 depicted the Messiah for us as the servant of God who would redeem us by incredible suffering, yet He would be the gentle loving shepherd as described in Psalm 23.

Our search for Him leads us into a spiritual journey that entails the conquest of fear, anxiety and all sinfulness in ourselves as we saw in Psalms 27 and 30. We also learn the joy of repentance and forgiveness in Psalms 32 and 51, as we struggle to pray and know Him better in Psalms 42 and 43, while learning how to offer to God true worship in Psalm 50. We discover that trust in God is the eye of the storm in Psalm 62, while our longing for deeper intimacy grew in Psalm 63. Desolation is part of our experience of God, as we saw in Psalm 88, and we discovered our need for protection on the journey in Psalm 91. Consolation follows on desolation in a new encounter with God in Psalm 95, and it leads us to one of our peak moments in Psalm 96. The whole experience revealed God's incredible love to us in Psalm 103, and to a deeper sense of His greatness when we discover a new depth of our own nothingness in Psalm 113. This sends us on our way singing a new pilgrim song in Psalm 121, and we learn the wisdom of keeping our eyes on the Lord in Psalm 123. The great liberation from the domination of the self is celebrated in Psalm 126, while we surrender to the Lord as the master builder of Church and state in Psalm 127. Now serene joy is ours as we let God be God for us and for everyone else in Psalm 131, and celebrate the wonder of our own creation in Psalm 139. Then at last we can join the universal grand finale of earth and heaven in the last choruses of the Psalter as the redeemed and joy-filled children of God.

Alleluia!

Praise God in his holy place,
praise him in his mighty heavens.
Praise him for his powerful deeds,
praise his surpassing greatness.

O praise him with sound of trumpet,
praise him with lute and harp.
Praise him with timbrel and dance,
praise him with strings and pipes.

O praise him with resounding cymbals,
praise him with clashing of cymbals.
Let everything that lives and that breathes
give praise to the Lord. Alleluia!

(vv. 1–6).

Present in the sanctuary or the house of God, the redeemed community, united with all creation and with the
heavenly hosts, stand to sing the last solemn Halleluia
Chorus that is the final response from man to God, a song
as everlasting as the goodness and mercy of God that
caused it. It is as if God had said to the covenant community
that was ready now for the revelation of Messiah in the Old
Testament, and to the Church, ready now for the second
coming of Jesus: "Arise, my beloved, my beautiful one,
and come! For see, the winter is past, the rains are over and
gone. The flowers appear on the earth . . . the song of the
dove is heard in our land. . . . Arise, my beloved, my
beautiful one, and come!"

The response is that community and creation arise as one
harnessing all the instruments of music in order to express
its exultation in being created, sustained, called, chosen
and redeemed, by so great a God as the father of Israel.
Since all has been said, it remains only to give the standing
ovation in a sustained fortissimo of praise. The inanimate
musical instruments lend power, volume and drama to the
swelling hearts of men and women who are lost in praise
and wonder, thanksgiving and joy.

The Book of Revelation gives us a glimpse into Heaven
in chapter 5, where the scene is very similar to this. All
Heaven had its eyes trained on Him who sits upon the
throne, and on the Lamb. The chorus of praise began with

four animals who prostrated themselves before the throne and the twenty-four elders who sang a new hymn to the Lamb: "You are worthy to take the scroll and break the seals of it, because you were sacrificed, and with your blood you bought men for God of every race, language, people and nation and made them a line of kings and priests to serve our God and to rule the world." This was the proclamation of praise that won an ecstatic response from all the dwellers of heaven. An immense number of angels responded first with shouts of praise: "The Lamb that was sacrificed is worthy to be given power, riches, wisdom, strength, honour, glory and blessing." This response of the angels was taken up by all living things including animals and humans who declared: "To the One sitting upon the throne and to the Lamb, be all praise, honour, glory and power, for ever and ever" (J.B.).

Epilogue

In this short book I have shared with you less than one third of the psalms, and I have not tried to cover all the themes to be found in the Psalter. To do so would require a much bigger work than the present one. I have limited myself to following some of the psalms which throw light on the various stages of the spiritual life, psalms which deal with the most common difficulties to be found along the way. It is wonderful to realize that men who lived two thousand five hundred years ago can still share the riches of their lives with us. This is because the psalms have divine inspiration, because their message is universal in its scope and so true to authentic human experience.

Perhaps you will be able to extract the messages from the rest of the psalms when you see the different ways in which I have approached them. There are many ways to deal with the psalms. One of the most popular is to take a theme and go through the whole Psalter finding out what it teaches on this subject. We can also look for the prophetic verses which are scattered throughout the Psalter. This leads us to research the New Testament in order to find the fulfilment of the prophecies, which can be exciting. And there are other ways too.

Nevertheless there is no substitute for quiet, deep, meditative reading of the psalms, especially in the presence of God, where we allow the Holy Spirit to enlighten us to the fuller meaning of the verses before us. As we learn to apply the lessons of the psalms to our lives we will experience their life-giving quality, for we will grow in wisdom and understanding as we allow God's Word to guide our lives into all truth.

Fount Paperbacks

Fount is one of the leading paperback publishers of religious books and below are some of its recent titles.

- ☐ THE WAY OF ST FRANCIS Murray Bodo £2.50
- ☐ GATEWAY TO HOPE Maria Boulding £1.95
- ☐ LET PEACE DISTURB YOU Michael Buckley £1.95
- ☐ DEAR GOD, MOST OF THE TIME YOU'RE QUITE NICE Maggie Durran £1.95
- ☐ CHRISTIAN ENGLAND VOL 3 David L Edwards £4.95
- ☐ A DAZZLING DARKNESS Patrick Grant £3.95
- ☐ PRAYER AND THE PURSUIT OF HAPPINESS Richard Harries £1.95
- ☐ THE WAY OF THE CROSS Richard Holloway £1.95
- ☐ THE WOUNDED STAG William Johnston £2.50
- ☐ YES, LORD I BELIEVE Edmund Jones £1.75
- ☐ THE WORDS OF MARTIN LUTHER KING Coretta Scott King (Ed) £1.75
- ☐ BOXEN C S Lewis £4.95
- ☐ THE CASE AGAINST GOD Gerald Priestland £2.75
- ☐ A MARTYR FOR THE TRUTH Grazyna Sikorska £1.95
- ☐ PRAYERS IN LARGE PRINT Rita Snowden £2.50
- ☐ AN IMPOSSIBLE GOD Frank Topping £1.95
- ☐ WATER INTO WINE Stephen Verney £2.50

All Fount paperbacks are available at your bookshop or newsagent, or they can be ordered by post from Fount Paperbacks, Cash Sales Department, G.P.O. Box 29, Douglas, Isle of Man, British Isles. Please send purchase price, plus 15p per book, maximum postage £3. Customers outside the U.K. send purchase price, plus 15p per book. Cheque, postal or money order. No currency.

NAME (Block letters) _____

ADDRESS _____

_____

While every effort is made to keep prices low, it is sometimes necessary to increase them at short notice. Fount Paperbacks reserve the right to show new retail prices on covers which may differ from those previously advertised in the text or elsewhere.